MORE PRAISE FOR *TRANS KIDS, OUR KIDS*

"Anti-LGBTQ+ forces are doing everything they can to dehumanize LGBTQ+ families and challenge our right to exist—and recently, they've had some success when it comes to transgender youth and their families. But we must never allow our community members, especially our courageous young people, to feel erased, ignored, or dismissed. And that's why *Trans Kids, Our Kids* is such an impactful book. It centers the stories of transgender young people—their challenges, triumphs, joys, and fears. It is only through honest and authentic storytelling like the stories featured in this book that we will be able to move our country toward a future where all of us can not just survive but thrive."—**Jaymes Black**, President and CEO, Family Equality

"Being visible as a transgender person during such a hostile time can be scary—but it can be an empowering opportunity to speak out and fight back against oppression. I so admire the trans young people and their loved ones who are speaking out in *Trans Kids, Our Kids*, which beautifully leverages in-depth personal narratives to capture the complexities of our current political moment."—**Aydian Dowling**, co-founder, Point of Pride

"Children are our future, plain and simple, and unfortunately we are living in a time where it is increasingly challenging to be a kid in the United States—especially an LGBTQ+ kid forced to navigate aggressive new laws and unprecedented attacks on books that represent their identities and lived experiences. I'm glad that *Trans Kids, Our Kids* exists to expertly document these challenges while also providing examples of a better path forward—one where all children, including trans children, are met with love, support, and respect."—**Isabel Galupo**, Emmy-nominated television writer and co-author of *Maiden and Princess*

"*Trans Kids, Our Kids* commits to elevating and amplifying the voices of trans young people and the many people who love them—reminding us of their power, courage, and strength. This book is an engrossing, essential exploration of our current moment in the LGBTQ+ movement."—**Andrea "Andy" Hong Marra**, Chief Executive Officer, Advocates for Trans Equality

"When the laws of your own state treat you as less than equal and block you from your hopes, dreams, and full potential, you have to push back and speak out—and that's exactly what so many young people, their parents, and community leaders dare to do in *Trans Kids, Our Kids*. I am in awe of the families and advocates featured in this book, who are doing everything they can to support their children, build supportive spaces, and empower young people to live with authenticity and dignity."
—**Jim Obergefell**, co-author, *Love Wins*, plaintiff in the Supreme Court marriage equality decision, *Obergefell v. Hodges*

"In the wake of an unprecedented wave of anti-trans legislation, *Trans Kids, Our Kids* provides a unique, invaluable window into the ways that families of transgender youth are grappling with the impossible choices imposed on them by these laws. Written by advocates who are actively on the frontlines, this book is a sobering illustration of the urgent demand for action."
—**Hannah Murphy Winter**, author, *Queer Power Couples: On Love and Possibility*

"This highly readable book is an excellent example of how to advance the conversation, engage one another, and continue making progress toward more inclusive lives and communities in all fifty states."—**Evan Wolfson**, Freedom to Marry founder and author of *Why Marriage Matters*

TRANS KIDS, OUR KIDS

Trans Kids, Our Kids

STORIES AND RESOURCES FROM THE FRONTLINES OF THE MOVEMENT FOR TRANSGENDER YOUTH

Alexis Stratton, Adam Polaski, and Jasmine Beach-Ferrara

New York, NY

Ig Publishing
Box 2547
New York, NY 10163
www.igpub.com

ISBN: 978-1-63246-167-4

PRINTED IN THE UNITED STATES OF AMERICA

FIRST EDITION | FIRST PRINTING

CONTENTS

To trans and gender nonconforming kids, their parents and caregivers, and everyone working to create spaces where all young people can thrive.

To N. and E.

To M.E.P. and T.P.

Acknowledgment of Indigenous Land

The Campaign for Southern Equality humbly acknowledges that all our work across the South is on Indigenous land. We are specifically based in Buncombe County, North Carolina, where we are on the ancestral land of the Cherokee. The Cherokee people inhabited more than 100,000 square miles across the Southeast. This land was acquired through violence, oppression, coercion, and broken treaties. We recognize the direct correlation between the loss of Indigenous people and land and the creation of the cities and the infrastructures that many of us use today. We also recognize the correlation between the loss of Indigenous lifeways and the colonial introduction of anti-LGBTQ+ sentiment that are some of the roots of many of the policies we fight today.

More than just acknowledging the past, we honor the continued presence and power of Indigenous people, and we commit to continued work and relationship-building with people and groups in our area and beyond.

Authors' Notes

1. Language around LGBTQ+ communities is ever-evolving and transforming. Over time, new words have emerged—and will continue to emerge—that describe gender identity, gender expression, sexual orientation, and other related identities in more nuanced ways—and we celebrate that. In the meantime, the language in this book reflects some of the best practices around LGBTQ+ terminology as of early 2024. Furthermore, as often as possible, we use the same words our interviewees use to define and describe themselves. Though we're stuck here in 2024, we can't wait to see what trans and queer futures lay ahead of us—and the wonderful words they will bring our way.
2. Similarly, as of April 2024, conversations are ongoing about best practices regarding the capitalization (or not) of racial identities, especially White. There are many reasons for not capitalizing white: as Mike Laws

at the *Columbia Journalism Review* wrote, "For many people, Black reflects a shared sense of identity and community. White carries a different set of meanings; capitalizing the word in this context risks following the lead of white supremacists."[1] However, we follow in the footsteps of the *Diversity Style Guide*, National Association of Black Journalists, Center for the Study of Social Policy, and other BIPOC writers, researchers, and journalists in capitalizing all racial and ethnic identities, including White.[2] As Ann Thúy Nguyễn and Maya Pendleton of the Center for the Study of Social Policy noted, "We believe that it is important to call attention to White as a race as a way to understand and give voice to how Whiteness functions in our social and political institutions and our communities. Moreover, the detachment of 'White' as a proper noun allows White people to sit out of conversations about race and removes accountability from White people's and White institutions' involvement in racism."[3] As we continue working and writing, though, we remain open to these conversations and best practices—and will continue adapting as they evolve.

3. The narratives in this book represent individual and/or family stories shared with us over the course of one or more interviews, and we have worked to accurately record and narrate those stories here. Some interviewees'

information, especially information about youth, has been anonymized to protect their privacy, including the use of several pseudonyms.

4. Throughout the book, we have noted when interview subjects use multiple pronouns. This is not to exceptionalize them (though we think trans and queer people are exceptional!) but for clarity and ease of reading, particularly as we often switch between pronouns when sharing these interviewees' stories.
5. The legal landscape for transgender youth is rapidly changing. Even as we wrote and edited this book in early 2024, new anti-trans laws were passed, and we worked to keep the information we shared as up to date as possible. Please note that by the time this book is in your hands, rulings may have been made in key cases mentioned in the chapters that follow, and other laws may have been passed (or overturned).
6. In the stories we share, there is some discussion of self-harm, suicide, bullying, discrimination, familial rejection, and physical violence, which may be distressing for some readers. The discussion of these topics is intended to foster understanding and empathy, but please be mindful of your own mental health while engaging with this content.
7. If you or someone you know is struggling with suicidal thoughts or behaviors, please seek help immediately.

You are not alone, and there are resources available to support you.

- If you are thinking about hurting yourself, call the National Suicide Prevention Lifeline at 1-800-273-TALK (8255).
- If you are an LGBTQ+ youth who is thinking about hurting yourself or is in crisis, call The Trevor Project's 24-Hour Suicide Prevention Hotline at 866-488-7386.
- If you are a transgender person in crisis or needing support, call Trans Lifeline at 877-565-8860.

Introduction

"Are you a girl or a boy?"

The first time I (Alexis) remember being asked this question, I was in third grade. I'd cut my hair super short for the first—but not the final—time, and whenever I met new kids, they didn't know which gender box to put me in.

When I was born, the doctor said I was a girl. But from a young age, I remember wishing that I wasn't. It was the early 1990s, and my mother assured me that a woman could be anything she wanted to. So, she let me dress how I wanted (in fourth grade, it was combat boots and baggy shorts and, occasionally, suspenders or a tie). She let me cut my hair. And she let me be bold and brash.

In the sixth grade, I wanted to play basketball at my school in rural Illinois—but the school only had a boys' team. My mom told me about Title IX (a 1972 law that requires schools to offer equivalent opportunities for boys' and girls' sports teams[1]), so I convinced a gaggle of girls to try out for the boys' team. The first year, no girls made it. The second year, one did. By the third year, the school had enough interested girls to form a girls' basketball team—and the girls' volleyball team became co-ed. My mom and I counted this as a success.

Yet, despite my mother's flexible notion of gender roles (especially for 1990s rural Illinois), questions of gender and identity continued to dog me. Eventually, I came out as queer while living in South Carolina in my late twenties (and cut my hair short for the fourth and forever time). But it wasn't until I started identifying as nonbinary in my early thirties that things seemed to click. Since then, I've often wondered if I'd had the words sooner, or a community of support sooner, would I have had a deeper understanding of myself sooner, too? If I had even an inkling of what "nonbinary" was, would I have seen it—and owned it—in myself from a young age?

•

We are living through a time of unprecedented support for LGBTQ+ equality. Recent studies have shown that an overwhelming majority of Americans favor marriage equality (71 percent), workplace equality (93 percent), and nondiscrimination protections (76 percent) for LGBTQ+ people.[2,3] This is the kind of support that can't be put back in the box and will only increase over time. Simultaneously, the past decade has been marked by waves of anti-trans and, more broadly, anti-LGBTQ+ bills and policies across the United States. According to the American Civil Liberties Union, in 2023, 510 anti-LGBTQ+ bills were proposed in forty-eight states.[4] Among these, eighty-four passed into law. (This compares to forty-seven anti-LGBTQ+ bills considered in the United States in all of 2018.[5]) Alarmingly, these numbers continue to rise, with 484 anti-LGBTQ+ bills proposed in state legislatures in forty states in the first four months of 2024.[6]

As these discriminatory policies are proposed—and passed—it often feels like a Category Five hurricane that builds off the coast, hits land, and then sweeps across one state after another—Mississippi, Tennessee, the Carolinas, Alabama, Arkansas, and on and on—until its impact has been felt by the entire LGBTQ+ community nationwide.

But the real target of most of these policies and laws are kids. Specifically, trans kids.

This is no accident. In recent years, conservative political forces in this country have engaged in a calculated and strategic effort to bulldoze every pillar of support that makes trans and queer youthhood survivable, including Gender-Sexuality Alliance (GSA) clubs in schools, affirming healthcare providers, books and media featuring LGBTQ+ characters, sports teams, and even supportive families. In Texas, the Department of Family and Protective Services has opened investigations into parents for loving and supporting their transgender children by letting them live as their full, authentic selves.[7] In Florida, a police report was filed against a school library for providing youth with books about LGBTQ+ and Black and Brown experiences.[8] An onslaught of gender-affirming care bans (sometimes with criminal penalties for parents or healthcare providers) is leaving families scrambling to find trans-related healthcare for their children. In more than two dozen states, legislatures have passed laws requiring school athletes to compete on teams that match their biological sex, effectively banning trans youth from participating in school sports. In many states, these laws have passed despite there being only one or two known transgender student athletes in the entire state—essentially putting a target specifically on their backs.[9]

Bills have also been signed into law restricting school bathroom access for transgender youth; making it more difficult for trans people to update government and legal documents with their affirmed gender; and codifying "sex" to refer to immutable biological sex characteristics.[10] Many of these laws impact LGBTQ+ youth more broadly, from the notorious "Don't Say LGBTQ+" laws that originated in Florida to preemption laws that prohibit cities or schools from adopting progressive LGBTQ+ policies. While these laws are being passed, the trans community is underrepresented at nearly all levels of government, with only a handful of out transgender people serving as state legislators and no out trans representatives in the US Congress.

The competing trajectories between the anti-LGBTQ+

movement and the large majority of Americans who support us will lead to either rupture or reconciliation—mirroring larger and escalating tensions in our country. These tensions cannot hold indefinitely; something will eventually have to give.

•

Expressions of queer or trans identities among young people have long been sources of conflict within families and communities, sparking fights over clothing choices, toys, activities, and, perhaps most painfully, over a child's early, instinctive ways of being who they are—how their voice sounds, how they move their bodies, and the adults they see and want to emulate. This has often led to isolation and exclusion for LGBTQ+ youth, and the internalization of a message that there is something essential about who they are that must be hidden. However, decades of organizing at political and community levels, steady progress at the judicial and legislative levels, progressive faith teachings, and advances in science and medicine have all altered the landscape that American children are being raised in. And because of such advancements, queer and trans people today experience more protection under the law than they ever have. Thus, many young people who in the past would have been condemned or told to hide their identities are instead expressing them at school, within their families, and in their faith communities with the full support of their loved ones, teachers, coaches, and faith leaders. Trans and queer identities are not new—they are, arguably, as old as humanity itself—but the ability to name and express these identities and, in many cases be met with support, is.

Those who oppose LGBTQ+ equality interpret this sea change as yet another sign of the degradation of mores in our country, and they have responded by attempting to police young people's bodies, modes of expression, conduct, sources of support, and more. The end result is what is happening in the United States as we write this book in early 2024—a desperate conservative backlash calculated to punish trans and queer young people by achieving maximal political impact in local, state, and federal elections. In 2014, *TIME Magazine* wrote that we were at a "transgender tipping point"; almost three years later, a young transgender child was featured on the cover of *National Geographic* under the headline "Gender Revolution."[11,12] Yet, anyone who thought we were in a post-gender (and post-racial, and post-feminist) country has surely been disabused of that notion by political developments of the past few years.

Transgender people, who during the freedom to marry movement were not typically the focus, have now been forced into this spotlight. Transgender issues are front and center in the body politic, being used as a political tool in elections up and down the ballot, playing out in debates around school curriculum, and being the subject of dozens of federal lawsuits.

The history of this can be traced back to morality laws and efforts to criminalize the expression of gender and sexuality—among LGBTQ+ people, but also among straight and cisgender (non-transgender) people—that reach back centuries. But the cruelty of the current attacks has stopped us in our tracks and filled us with rage and grief. To make children the target of such hate and to expend such enormous political resources to attack them is a heartbreaking travesty.

•

The marriage equality fight that led to the 2015 Supreme Court decision requiring states to issue marriage licenses to same-gender couples was responsible for one of the fastest transformations in public opinion in recorded history (from 27 percent support of marriage equality in 1996 to 71 percent support in 2023).[13] Behind this swift change in belief were the many stories that same-gender couples and their family members shared with the public. Hearing about these relationships, understanding their stories, and contextualizing them in the universal language of love, commitment, trust, and respect helped fuel people's support for marriage equality across the country.

In contrast, when it comes to transgender equality, much of the discourse has left out the real lived experiences of transgender people and their partners, families, and communities. Far too often, and by design, trans people's experiences have been distilled down to which bathroom they will use and other misguided preoccupations with their bodies. Instead of support, young trans people who are seeking to express their fully actualized selves are medicalized and distorted through scare-tactic filters.

The main reason we wrote this book is to uplift the voices and stories of young trans people who are caught in the middle of the worst cultural polarization we've seen in our lifetimes—and who also, because of both their age and their trans identities, experience the very definition of political powerlessness. These are the voices of real people who are, day in and out, going about the stuff of life while also navigating the political firestorm directed at them.

In this book, we share snapshots of the struggles and triumphs of everyday Americans and their children who are living with the reality of anti-transgender and anti-queer laws, policies, and attitudes. From an Indian American family in Virginia grappling with transphobic bullying at school to a transgender attorney at a top law firm in New York City fighting against a gender-affirming care ban to a small but mighty group of trans activists who opened a community center in Arkansas, we have been honored to listen to the stories of people from almost every corner of the country who are living through the impacts of these laws. The stories they share paint a picture of resistance and resilience—of building community, advocating for change, and creating trans joy in the midst of such distressing times. Stories cut through the shrill, distorting political noise and may also be the best shot we have of finding our way through a perilous time in our country and, in the process—if we are lucky—finding each other along the way.

•

This project emerged from the intersections of our personal and political lives. Collectively, the three of us have decades of experience working on the frontlines (and in the background) of trans and queer justice movements. From founding the Campaign for Southern Equality (CSE), an organization which works toward legal and lived equality in the LGBTQ+ South, to providing community-based trainings on LGBTQ+ cultural competency, to leading communications and digital organizing efforts in states across the country, we have seen firsthand the challenges that LGBTQ+ Americans—both young and old—face.

Today, we all hold various roles at CSE, which has been rapidly responding to the emerging legal and personal challenges faced by transgender youth and their families. We are especially proud of one of our newest programs, which we launched in 2023 as the Southern Trans Youth Emergency Project (STYEP) in response to the passage of a wave of state-level bans on gender-affirming care in southern states.

Gender-affirming care can include a spectrum of health services that help transgender people align their physical, biological, interpersonal, and emotional traits with their gender identity;[14] most of the laws that have passed specifically ban or restrict medical care for minors, including hormone replacement therapy and puberty-blocking medications. As bans sprang up in 2022 and 2023 across the South—and beyond—our team and our partners leaped into action to help families navigate the maze of transgender healthcare by providing them with grants, patient navigation, education, and other resources. In summer 2024, CSE expanded the project (now called the Trans Youth Emergency Project, or TYEP) to serve trans youth and their families in any state with a ban on gender-affirming care (half of the states in the country, as of June 2024).

TYEP grew out of the needs expressed to us by trans youth and the people who support them—and would not be possible without the collaborative support of our community partners like QMed, OUTMemphis, Kentucky Health Justice Network, and many others featured in this book. As we do this work every day, we hear the stories of trans youth facing one barrier after another—and of the incredible lengths to which parents, providers, attorneys, and community organizations are going to help them. We want the world to hear these stories, too.

From January to April 2024, we interviewed more than fifty individuals who were diverse in terms of geography, age, race, class, gender, sexuality, ability, geography, socioeconomic status, and professional roles. Participants hailed from nineteen states and included a Filipino American youth activist in Ohio; a Salvadoran organizer in Arkansas; a Black minister in South Carolina; a Black Dominican American student at Yale University; a White transgender debate team star in Alabama; an Indigenous Two-Spirit activist in Oregon—and others. We also met with the parents of trans kids, which included non-LGBTQ+ married parents who had never met a trans person before they had a trans kid, parents who were themselves queer, single parents who adopted without a partner, and divorced parents. We learned from trans and queer activists doing intersectional work in Florida, North Carolina, South Carolina, Arkansas, Tennessee, and elsewhere. We spoke to cisgender and transgender attorneys, healthcare providers, advocates, and community members who are walking alongside young people as they navigate today's shifting terrain.

Even with this wide range of voices, we were not able to represent *every* story about transgender youth in the United States. There are experiences and narratives we have missed, and others we have not explored deeply enough. However, by contextualizing and sharing the stories we were able to gather, as well as offering next steps and resources, we hope to narrativize the pain and fear experienced by everyday people in this cultural moment—and to shine a bright light on the courage, hope, and resilience of trans and gender nonconforming youth, their families, and the people who love and support them.

Ultimately, this book is a collection of stories about love, just as it was stories about love that proved such a powerful accelerant in the movement for the freedom to marry. This is no coincidence, as all of this work is, at its core, about love and its power to free us, heal us, and change us.

This book features stories about the love of a parent who will—like so many parents—do anything to care for her child. The love of a community to invent, iterate, innovate, and invest in creating spaces of affirmation and support for children. The love of a doctor or lawyer, and their decision to fuse their passion and talents to help people achieve their dreams. The love of a sibling who just wants to jump on a trampoline with her brother, without the state constantly trying to hurt her family. And above all, the wonder of young transgender people striving so deeply to love themselves—even as they hear messages of disapproval and contempt from many corners of their lives.

Children should not have to fight so hard to express who they truly are. Children should never hear themselves being condemned by elected officials and faith leaders, nor have to live through the cruel and chaotic process of being targeted by discriminatory laws. Yet this is the reality that young trans people in the United States are living through—showing deep and remarkable reserves of courage and resolve as they do so. "To be yourself in a world that is constantly trying to make you something else," as the Ralph Waldo Emerson quote goes, "is the greatest accomplishment." The experience of this freedom is all the more powerful when you know that you are loved exactly as you are—and when you know you are not alone. Everyone deserves a love story. On the pages that follow, we are honored to share dozens of them with you.

PART I: INTO THE MAZE

Chapter One

Lauren Green wasn't taking "no" for an answer.

She and her seventeen-year-old daughter, Lydia, were in the middle of a five-and-a-half-hour drive from Oklahoma to Arkansas in January 2024 for a routine appointment with Lydia's doctor when a call came through on Lauren's phone. It was the doctor's office: "Are you sure you're coming?" the front desk worker asked. "Other clients are canceling, and we totally understand if you need to reschedule."

"No!" Lauren nearly started sobbing. "We. Will. *Be. There.*"

The office had already called once to confirm the appointment, due to the weather. All morning long, Lauren and Lydia had been driving through a snow and ice storm, and conditions were hazardous. "We basically drove behind the storm the whole time," Lauren says.

Lauren was determined to get Lydia to the appointment. It was time for her three-month checkup, where she could get her bloodwork, speak with her provider about anything that needed to be changed, and get a prescription for a refill on the medicine that she had been taking for over a year.

Lauren and Lydia usually only had to drive a few miles to see Lydia's doctor. But this time was different. That's because Lydia is transgender—and in October 2023, the state of Oklahoma began enforcing a law that prohibited minors from being prescribed or administered medicine used for gender transition. That meant Lydia could no longer receive care where they lived in Oklahoma, and the closest option was Arkansas, where a similar law had passed but was not in effect due to a federal court order.

The drive was already proving treacherous—and it wasn't just the weather. For one thing, Lauren and Lydia hadn't slept well the night before. They had to wake up early to ensure they could make the appointment with the clinic in Arkansas. Both of them were cranky. Lauren's brain ran through a litany of worries like ticker tape: What if the Arkansas-based provider wouldn't take their insurance? What if the weather prevented them from taking the trip? If that happened, when would they be able to reschedule, and would Lauren be able to pull Lydia out of school? Where would they go to get the medication filled in Arkansas, how long would it take, and what if the pharmacist gave them a hard time?

About halfway through the trip, Lydia expressed excitement about finishing the appointment and immediately heading back home. However, Lauren reminded her that they were staying the night in Little Rock. Lydia hadn't realized that—and tried her hardest to convince Lauren that they should drive straight home after the appointment. But Lauren was worried that if the appointment took longer than expected, they wouldn't have adequate time to call in the prescription, which was prohibited from being filled at an Oklahoma pharmacy. "We were both really discouraged," Lauren recalls.

On top of these stresses, the two of them held their breath every time they stopped to use the restroom in rural Arkansas, worried about what to do if someone gave them problems. Lydia noted during the drive how "scary and humiliating" it was to have to drive to another, even more conservative state—the first state to have passed an anti-transgender healthcare ban. "Everything built up, and it was really exhausting on every level—a nightmare," Lauren remembers.

Thankfully, the clinic stayed open for Lydia, who was the last patient of the day. "I was very grateful for that," Lauren says. "I would not have been able to handle it if we couldn't see her doctor that day."

In some ways, all these challenges made it feel like the deck was stacked against them—that the fates were sending signals that they did not want Lauren and Lydia to make this appointment. In other ways, it felt like a metaphor for their journey as a family: even with all the obstacles that littered their path, Lauren and Lydia could make it through, weather the literal storm, and come out the other side.

Lauren and Lydia came into each other's lives more than five years ago. Lauren had long known that she wanted to become a parent through adoption, and she adopted Lydia through the Oklahoma Department of Human Services (DHS). She looked through a book of children in need of homes and stopped on a page that included Lydia. Something felt right, and so DHS arranged to have the two meet at a local Starbucks.

"I nearly threw up from nerves so many times," Lauren says of their initial meeting. "I was so nervous—and Lydia was even more nervous." Lydia came and stayed with Lauren a few times before moving in on a more permanent basis—which happened to be the exact week that COVID-19's spread led to stay-at-home orders nationwide. For several weeks, Lauren and Lydia had nothing but time to get to know each other and become a family—the two of them and their cat, Marley. They bonded over video games, including a ton of *Mario Kart*, and while they didn't totally align in their tastes in TV shows or movies, they've learned over time to compromise. (On the "anniversary" of Lydia's move-in, she approached Lauren with a semi-begrudging olive branch: "I'll watch *Star Wars* with you.")

During their time together, Lydia also began opening up about her gender identity. "She started telling me about herself and how she wanted to be," Lauren remembers.

Now they have been a family for just over four years.

Lauren and Lydia had already been forced to relocate their

care once before. For two years, they had been seeing a provider at Oklahoma Children's Hospital at OU Health in Oklahoma City, which worked with them on a care plan that made sense for Lydia. Eventually, she began taking puberty blockers. By October 2022, Lydia was ready for her first round of gender-affirming hormone therapy, and they were scheduled for their first appointment on a Tuesday. On Monday of that week, however, Oklahoma Governor Kevin Stitt announced plans to sign an executive order specifically targeting OU Children's, withholding COVID-19 federal relief funds from the institution unless it stopped providing gender-affirming care to trans people under eighteen.[1] OU Children's is one of the state's largest hospital systems, and at the time, it was providing care to approximately 100 trans youth. "It was like *the place* in the state to go," Lauren says. "I remember thinking, we've worked so hard for this, my kid is so excited about this, and now our stupid governor is going to ruin it. That was the day my outrage finally spilled over."

Lauren had read about the executive order from social media posts by Freedom Oklahoma, the statewide organization that had been so helpful in the first two years of Lydia's transition, assisting with changing her name and providing access to a support group for Lauren. Anxious, she called OU Children's about their appointment—should they still plan on coming in? "Our lawyers have advised us that nothing is signed into law," the receptionist explained. "We will see patients right up until he signs it."

At the appointment, the doctor spent an hour in the exam room with Lydia before calling Lauren in to join them. Lauren opened the door to the room, and the first words she heard from the doctor were, "That motherfucker's not going to get us! We're going to get this done today, before he signs that." By the time Lauren and Lydia left the building, they had completed labs, a referral to a different clinic that could see them for their follow-up appointments, and Lydia had begun her first round of hormones.

It was both a triumphant and cold moment. Lauren explains, "It was so hard knowing that my kid was balanced between having such excitement about having just gotten the care she needed and the absolute terror that it was already going to be taken away."

The experience would become a familiar one for Lauren and Lydia; they've had to change providers four different times since Lydia began her medical transition. Lauren shares, "Every place we go, we say, 'If we lose access to you, what do we do next? Where do we go?'"

•

Ana Martínez has been up to her eyeballs in research about medical options for her child, August. They live in Alabama, where one of the earliest anti-transgender healthcare bans passed in June 2022. It is one of the few laws of its kind with felony penalties for providers of gender-affirming care. "I sent tons of letters, signed every petition I saw, tried to make Alabama politicians see that they did not need to pass this law," Ana remembers. The law initially took effect for seven days before a federal judge issued a preliminary injunction, meaning that he expected the law to be found unconstitutional.[2] Judge Liles C. Burke, who was appointed by President Trump, wrote, "Based on the record evidence, the Court finds that the imminent threat of harm to Parent Plaintiffs and Minor Plaintiffs—i.e., severe physical and/or psychological harm—outweighs the harm the State will suffer from the injunction."[2]

In the months that followed, Ana was on edge and unsure of what she would do to get August care. The status of Alabama's ban was difficult to track because of the inconstant drip of legal developments. But her provider was reassuring—and the court order prohibiting enforcement of the law was holding solid. Maybe the ban would never take effect again, they hoped. As state after state passed their own versions of anti-trans healthcare bans throughout 2023, it seemed like Alabama might remain a state with access, a function of early litigation. Ana thought that they had landed in a place of relative stability, where her son's care would remain accessible. "We were, like, in la-la land," she says. "I had stopped looking at the news. And we felt like we had our little safe haven here. But it wasn't that safe."

In March 2023, they arrived at their long-scheduled

three-month appointment, which August had reminded his mom about repeatedly. She needed to pull him out of school for the appointment, and he was excited to get his testosterone refill. But when they arrived at the doctor's office, they were told that the ban was in effect and his prescription was not legally allowed to be renewed.

At first, they were in shock—could they be exempt since they were already receiving care? Was the law definitely in effect? August broke down in tears. "He never cries," Ana shares. "It was heartbreaking to see him like that, with the doctor unable to help him. But I told the doctor that I was not going to leave my kid without the care he needed." Ana knew the positive impact that the medicine had on her child, with August feeling "extremely happy, more confident, and physically stronger."

In Alabama, young people are legally minors until they turn nineteen. So August still had a long road in front of him—more than three years. And his need was extremely urgent: August only had a few weeks left until his medicine would run out.

Ana quickly got to work. That same day, she contacted all her friends who lived in states with less oppressive healthcare laws, as well as several friends who were doctors. She was humbled by the support she received. A friend who was a doctor in New Jersey offered to ask all his contacts for referrals. A friend in Colorado invited Ana and August to stay at his place so that they could receive care nearby. Friends and family members in Minneapolis, Philadelphia, and Seattle also offered support.

When Ana found the website for the Campaign for Southern Equality's Southern Trans Youth Emergency Project (STYEP) and had a call with a patient navigator, she was able to add new possible locations to her list of potential providers.

As she called through the list, however, Ana kept running into obstacles. Some clinics didn't accept out-of-state patients, or they were limited to accepting patients who lived in a specific region. Some clinics had very long wait lists—far longer than the four-week window that Ana had to refill August's prescription. One clinic required the family to enlist another social worker for an additional letter diagnosing August with gender dysphoria. One clinic did not treat minors at all. Ana thought that a clinic in Pennsylvania made the most sense—but flights to the state were nearly $600 per person, and the trip would require at least a night or two of hotel costs.

Eventually, Ana decided that a permanent solution might not be possible. So, she registered August as a patient with QMed, a telehealth provider that specializes in gender-affirming care, and began planning for the four-and-a-half-hour drive out of state. As long as Ana and August could physically get themselves to a state without a ban, they would be able to see the telehealth provider.[3]

Ana distills the description of what it feels like to be a parent of a trans kid today down to one word: "Impotent." "I'm seeing my kid, who is only fifteen, struggling and suffering so much, and that is devastating for me," she says. "And we know what's best for him is the treatment that he was getting, with the doctors controlling everything. And now it feels like we're left helpless—like, you're on your own. Good luck."

•

Kenya Harris feels much the same way as Ana. "I mean, oh my goodness—this is my child," she says about her sixteen-year-old daughter, Ari, who is a transgender girl. "What are we supposed to do? It feels like they're just throwing us to the wolves, leaving me to figure out something that is already hard to navigate—and now making it that much harder."

Their situation is especially confusing and illustrates the randomness and heartbreaking absurdity of anti-trans laws. Kenya and Ari live in Newport, Kentucky, and from the time she was born, Ari received health care at Cincinnati Children's Hospital in Ohio. A gender-affirming care ban took effect in Kentucky in 2023,[4] but it didn't dramatically impact Ari, since she was receiving care in Ohio.

Then in January 2024, Ohio passed its own ban when the state legislature voted to override a veto from Republican Governor Mike DeWine. The Ohio law provides an exception for young people who initiated care prior to the law's enactment in April 2024—but *only* if the child is an Ohio resident. Despite living literally a four-minute drive from the border and being born in the state, Ari is now prohibited from receiving care at

Cincinnati Children's.

"Ari has always been Ari," Kenya shares. "Growing up, she kind of leaned more toward dolls and dollhouses and kitchen sets. And I supported her because that's what she wanted to do." Two weeks before Ari turned fourteen, just before starting high school, she came out to Kenya—sharing that she "felt like she was in the wrong body." Kenya wasn't totally shocked; in many ways, it made sense. But she didn't have a lot of knowledge on best practices for supporting transgender youth and didn't feel like there were many models that could help guide her. "Me being a young African American mother in total support of my [trans] daughter is something that is a bit unheard of where we come from," Kenya says. "But here we are!"

After Ari came out, Kenya shared the update with Ari's doctor, and they scheduled an appointment to talk about next steps. Over time, Ari began receiving gender-affirming hormone therapy. The doctors were a strong source of support for the family, pointing Kenya in the right direction in terms of resources and information about how best to support a transgender child.

Now, just because Kenya and Ari live on the other side of the river, they are ineligible to receive transition-related care in Ohio. It's a major loss. But in the lead-up to the ban taking effect, they still felt the love and support from Ari's doctors, who shared information with the family, including about resources that were available and other medical providers that might be able to see them. "They are still trying to do everything that they can legally," Kenya says.

It's not just the healthcare ban that the family is grappling with: last year when Kentucky's ban passed, it included a section that essentially amounted to a "Don't Say LGBTQ+" law, similar to the ones that have passed in Florida and North Carolina. Ari's school called a meeting with Kenya and explained that Ari would now be required to use a designated restroom and that, under the law, the school did not have to address Ari by her correct name or pronouns—although, they said, they would continue doing so. "Ari has a great rapport with the folks at school," Kenya says. "But it's tough to see these effects. It's like it's coming in waves."

The next wave is figuring out how to handle the time between now and Ari turning eighteen in July 2025. There's a lot of negotiation and number-crunching going through Kenya's mind. For example, Ari typically sees her provider every six months, so Kenya knows they'll need to take at least one trip out of state before she turns eighteen. But the closest destination with access is hundreds of miles away, which will be a financial and logistical challenge for the family. Kenya is trying to figure out if they can stretch their medicine supply or cobble together a treatment plan that works for them so that they can avoid a second trip out of state. "Something is better than nothing," she says.

While they sort out the specifics, they're trying to stay positive. "I am feeling some hope just seeing the light at the end of the tunnel and knowing that, eventually, we will come to a point where it'll be all right," Kenya says. "It's just taking it one step at a time, one day at a time, one moment at a time, and knowing that it will get better."

Kenya has also drawn strength from seeing how much support Ari has received from family members, close friends, her school, and her peers. "That's also given us hope—knowing that not everyone is against a person being who they want and need to be." Kenya and Ari are focused on remaining grateful—for the community that has supported them, for the resources helping them navigate this challenging time, and for each other. "My mom has always been my number one support system," Ari shares. "I just feel like we were truly a match made in heaven. Without her being my mother and my everything, I wouldn't be who I am today, literally and figuratively. I simply wouldn't be here."

•

For some families, the trans healthcare bans have been uniquely devastating, splitting them apart and making them feel like the only choice they have is to move to another state.

For several months now, Becca Robinson has been living 1,300 miles away from her husband Mike and their three children; their oldest child, Jaxon, is thirteen years old, and he is transgender. The family has always lived in Houston, Texas, but as policies from the Texas legislature and executive administration toward transgender youth became increasingly hostile, Becca and Mike kept their eyes open for opportunities that would allow them to leave the state.

In the fall of 2023, a position opened up at a hospital in San Diego, and Becca, a neonatal nurse, jumped at the chance. She got the job, and now she flies between San Diego and Houston while Mike works in Texas and looks after the kids. Becca has rented an apartment and is looking for homes to purchase, but the transition has been far from seamless, as Mike, an attorney, cannot find work in California until he takes the state's bar exam. And they have been unable to sell their house in Houston. "What we're experiencing has surprising parallels to a traditional refugee story, where the dad goes somewhere to establish a better life, and then the family comes later," Mike explains. "We would do anything for our kids, but the fact that we are essentially refugees within the United States is mind-blowing."

Becca remembers when it fully crystallized for her that they'd have to leave Texas. In the summer of 2023, she was in the grocery store when she received a call from Jaxon's doctor, who told her he wouldn't be able to see Jaxon any longer for transition-related care. Texas had passed a trans healthcare ban that wasn't set to take effect until September 1 of that year, but the provider, like nearly all providers statewide, was ceasing care early for fear of retaliation or investigation from the state government. "I couldn't really believe it was happening," Becca says. "But at that point, I was like, 'We have to get the eff out of Texas.'" Other policies in the state already deeply concerned her, including the state's abortion ban and high maternal mortality rate. She saw so many medical crises in her work as a neonatal intensive care unit nurse. "That politics is practicing medicine is just insane to me—it's barbaric," she says. "We cannot stay here. It's not safe. And it's not somewhere I want to raise my family."

When their Houston-based provider stopped care for trans youth, they shared informational resources with Becca and Mike about potential options for continuing Jaxon's care. Becca and Mike considered Mt. Sinai in New York City, where Becca has family with whom they could stay during visits for appointments, and UCSF Medical Center in San Francisco. UCSF had availability sooner than Mt. Sinai, but it still took months to get an appointment for Jaxon.

Becca and Jaxon took their first trip together to California in the fall of 2023. Prior to the flight, Becca and Mike tried to shelter Jaxon as best as they could from what was happening, not wanting to scare him. "The emotional burden is a lot, but we were trying to keep a happy face," Becca shares.

The medical care team at UCSF was very friendly and caring, and Becca couldn't help feeling moved by the sympathy and even pity they felt for her family. "I'm so sorry you're having to go through this," the doctor told the family. "Jaxon, I want you to know that we love you here. We care about you. And you're a boy, and I'm sorry that you live in Texas where they don't recognize that."

Becca also learned that the doctor was afraid for the family's safety. At 6:00 the morning after their appointment, the day that Becca and Jaxon were set to fly home, Becca received a call on her cell phone from the doctor. Her voice sounded heavy. "I'm worried about you trying to get your lab work done in Texas," the doctor said. "If there's any way that you can possibly get it done this morning before you go back to Texas, I would really like that—I just worry it will raise some red flags if you get it done at home."

Becca found a lab that could complete the bloodwork, and a few hours later, she and Jaxon boarded their flight. While they were in the air, Jaxon turned to his mom. "I didn't realize how bad it is in Texas," he said. "The doctors really seemed to think we live in a different country." He chuckled at that, but Becca thought she saw the weight of the situation sink in a bit more in her child's mind. "That was really a pivotal moment for him—when he realized, like, 'Oh my gosh, we do have to leave.'"

Since the trip, the Robinsons have had to take or plan for additional journeys to San Francisco for Jaxon's care, which causes multiple challenges for the family. First, one of the parents has to take time off from work. They also have to pull Jaxon out of school, telling administrators that he's sick. "I have integrity," Becca says. "But at this point, my integrity and values lie with my child. And I can't say that we're going out of state for a doctor's appointment—that would be so risky, with the state government already trying to make examples of families. We're having to make these decisions and changes that we don't want to make."

Costs are also an issue. "We went from a fifty-five dollar copay at the office down the street to having to book two flights, a hotel room, and take Jaxon out of school. It went from a fifty-five dollar copay to a $2,000 nightmare," Mike says. "Flying to San Francisco and back in a day so that a doctor can look at Jaxon for thirty minutes so that he can keep getting his medication, which we're now having to smuggle into Texas, is absurd—all for treatment that is acknowledged as necessary and medically recommended."

Despite the hurdles, Mike and Becca are trying to stay focused on what's most important: the health and well-being of their child. "We're lucky enough that we can afford to do all of this, but doing it while not saddling Jaxon with any sense of these things being his fault . . . that takes a constant, vigilant effort," Mike says. "There's enough that comes along with raising a thirteen-year-old without adding all of these external factors."

•

The thought of moving has come up for many parents of transgender kids living in states with healthcare bans. For Erica

Barker, it seemed like the only real option. She is the mother of fourteen-year-old twins—Mylah, who is transgender, and Max, who has recently come out as nonbinary. The family has lived in Jackson, Mississippi, for the entirety of the twins' lives, but Erica and her husband Rick felt certain that getting their two LGBTQ+ kids through the next few years in a political climate like Mississippi's would be like trying to square a circle.

At the end of 2023, the family moved to Las Vegas, Nevada. It's Erica's favorite city in the country—the place where she and Rick got married, where they like to vacation, where they like the weather, and most importantly, where LGBTQ+-affirming policies are relatively strong.

Like the Robinsons, Erica, Rick, and the kids moved in stages. Rick arrived first, in September, buying a house and getting it ready for his family. For the rest of the fall, Erica juggled the busy schedules of her then thirteen-year-olds and made arrangements to prepare for the rest of the move. It was all exhausting—and extremely expensive. "The move has cost us about $50,000," Erica says. "I'm afraid to go back and add everything else up because it would probably be much more than that, and I wouldn't be able to handle it. My husband and I are pretty fiscally responsible, even frugal. But by no stretch of the imagination are we rich folks."

Rick served for twenty-three years in the United States Army and is now retired due to disability. He's lived all over the country and around the world—and last year, he celebrated his twentieth year in remission from leukemia, which resulted in his disability status. "He is doing well but can only do certain types of work, and he can only make a certain amount of money," Erica says. Being home allows Rick to provide childcare for the twins—and also be available for the family's twenty-six-year-old daughter.

Erica and Rick took to the daunting task of moving in a methodical manner. First, they considered what to do with their home. The housing market was not ideal in Jackson, and the Barkers weren't sure what to do with their house if they couldn't sell it—should they try to rent it and maintain the two mortgages in two states?

Next, they turned to the kids' schooling. They knew that Clark County, Nevada, where they were moving, had a reputation for inadequate public education, so they had to decide whether they'd move their children from the public schools of Jackson to a private school near their new home in Nevada.

Third, they had to go about the act of physically moving—themselves, their furniture and belongings, and their fifteen-pound cat.

And finally, they had to come up with cash for the deposit on their rental house in Las Vegas and to cover utilities and payments for two homes, all in addition to their regular bills.

On top of all those expenses were the costs associated with starting Mylah on transition-related medication. In the early days of the healthcare bans, Erica drove Mylah to Birmingham,

Alabama, to begin her care there. The care was prohibitively expensive—and even if it wasn't, driving into Alabama made Erica nervous. In Mississippi, the state anti-trans law officially carries a clause prohibiting the "aiding and abetting" of procuring gender-affirming care. The intentionally vague language has left many families uncertain about their rights and fearful about whether an overzealous attorney general or governor could try to target them.

Meanwhile, the family was also paying for therapy sessions for both Mylah and Max. Their insurance only officially covered four therapy sessions total for dependents, but Erica was able to push for more, eventually landing at eight sessions total—four for Mylah and four for Max. Additional appointments amounted to an out-of-pocket expense.

All these expenses and logistical challenges have been worth it, Erica and Rick say, as there is no doubt in their minds that Mylah needs this care. "I don't really think she had a coming out period," Erica says. "We've always known her to be this dynamic butterfly." But at age seven, Mylah did approach Erica and Rick and tell them, "I think I'm somebody else, and I want to try to explore that, because that's going to make me happy." A little while later, Max asserted their nonbinary identity. After this, Erica and Rick enrolled their kids in therapy and signed up for their own family therapy. "That was the foundation," Erica says. "Once we were certain this was the path the twins were going to take, we did everything we could to support them."

Mylah coming out as transgender also stirred a further drive and motivation in Erica to get more involved in social justice and to advocate for her children and people like them. "I've got to get up to speed on these issues," she says—and what better way than to apply for a job at the ACLU of Mississippi? The organization was hiring for a paralegal, so Erica brushed off her legal chops, interviewed, and got the job.

As an ACLU of Mississippi employee, Erica became hyper-aware of the legislation that was being considered in Mississippi that would impact her family—including bills related to LGBTQ+ identity and racial justice; her family is African American, and the Mississippi legislature was as racist as it was anti-LGBTQ+. She also heard rumblings that anti-transgender legislation was coming down the pipeline. "Still, I was hoping that they wouldn't sign anti-transgender policies into law," Erica recalls. "I felt like we would be on heightened alert, and that they would carry a big stick—but I honestly thought we'd just continue to fight this thing until the kids turned eighteen, and then we'd get them out of here and strongly encourage them to go to college out of state, somewhere else."

Healthcare bans in the state were first introduced in 2020 and 2021, and that's when she and Rick seriously started considering what a move could look like. The next year, Erica pulled Rick aside again. "I know we've talked about the possibility," she shared. "But let's stop speaking hypothetically. Let's start looking at some things. Let's look at our finances.

Let's figure out how we can make this work."

It wasn't just the potential for the medical care ban—Mylah and Max were also facing issues at school, including misgendering and disrespect from teachers and administrators, bullying from peers, and being told they didn't have the right to exist. "My kids have been called the N-word and the F-word at the same time," Erica says. "I would pick them up from school, and Mylah would always be in tears. And every day on the ride home I would have that same conversation with her: 'Mylah, you're more than good enough. Mylah, you don't owe anyone anything.'"

Things are better now in Nevada. Mylah doesn't cry every day anymore. Erica, Rick, and the kids like to take walks, and they only have to drive a short distance to get to the mountains. "Mylah's always like, 'This is a green screen,'" Erica says, thrilled that her kids feel connected to nature. Erica's also been able to keep the job she loves at the ACLU, working remotely and taking occasional trips back to Jackson.

The new school has been a major improvement. Upon enrollment, the school administration held a gender support team meeting with Erica and Rick, and they filled out forms with Mylah's chosen name, which will follow her throughout her academic career.

Still, it's not perfect. There's still some bullying. And Erica has struggled to identify or connect with strong community supports. She is especially eager to connect with other Black families with LGBTQ+ kids, especially transgender children. "I know we're out here—but why aren't there more outlets specifically for African American youth?" she asks. "When you have experienced trauma, you often find comfort in individuals that look like you. I'm interested and hungry to find that kind of connection, so I can understand whether the challenges we've experienced are unique to us or are similar to what other families of color have gone through."

Erica is trying to take her own advice to her kids—to be patient and realize that "there is not one fix for everything." She understands that progress sometimes happens one (slow) step at a time. She's seen it in her own family: her mother routinely misgenders Max and Mylah and has struggled to accept their gender identity, referring to them as The Boys. "She has the biggest heart—but that's extremely hurtful to me," Erica says. In February 2024, however, Erica's mom sent the twins birthday cards. Mylah's card featured a glittery pink unicorn. "That's a big win," Erica told Mylah. "We've got some baby steps!"

"She's trying—and that's all we ask of anybody," Erica says of her mother. "If you got to know these kids, they're such beautiful souls. You would see that this is not something that's been imposed on them, or a lifestyle or identity that they chose. This is who they are."

Erica also derives a lot of strength from her faith. "I acknowledge every day that we didn't get here all on our own," she says. "We're in the right place because our steps have already been ordered. I have faith in a higher power that has made all of us who we are. And when you're doing what's best for your child's well-being and your family, it's just the right decision. I was so excited to be able to make this move, and it's been right for my family." Erica starts to cry. "But Jackson is home. And I miss my sisters. And I miss my mom."

Erica and Rick lived right across the street from one of her sisters, and her other sister lived around the corner, two streets away. The proximity allowed them to celebrate birthdays together and have big family dinners. Erica became the host for Thanksgiving while her sister across the street hosted Christmas and the sister two blocks away hosted New Year's Eve. "My sisters get on my nerves and vice versa, but those girls are my best friends," she says.

Together, the siblings cared for their father, who was terminally ill and took a turn for the worse six years ago. They shared responsibilities for his care. They mourned his death together.

Erica remembered when she and Rick bought their house in Jackson in 2015. When they closed, her dad came over to congratulate them. "He was such a very proud man—kind of rough around the edges, kind of stoic," Erica shares. "Everybody had massive respect for him. He was the kind of person who, if people needed advice or guidance, they called him." He gave Erica and Rick an envelope—just a little something to help out with the inherent expenses of a new home, he said. Erica figured it was a little bit of cash, maybe $100. She didn't open it for a few weeks, and when she did, she saw that there was a check for several thousand dollars and a card that said, *I am so proud of you.* "My sisters and I took a great deal of pride in making our dad proud or happy for us," Erica says. "And he bragged to everyone about us being able to buy that house. He bragged to his friends that all of his girls were right there in the same neighborhood. He was so happy. So having to leave that house—the house that we worked so very hard to get, the house that we earned, the house that my dad was so proud of us for . . . that was the most difficult thing to leave. When the moving truck pulled away from our house, that's what got me the most out of everything—that I'm leaving this place that brought my dad such a great sense of pride. And you can't put a dollar amount on that."

•

Despite the stories of families like the Barkers and Robinsons who leave their states, many families do not want to go anywhere else, no matter how hostile the environment has become for trans youth.

The day Governor Stitt announced he would be signing the executive order disrupting their access to Oklahoma University Health, Lauren Green admitted that she started researching her options, looking at maps of where health care was accessible to trans youth and where she might be able to get a job. "I just thought, we can't stay here, we're going to have to move," she explains. "It's going to be really different and more expensive, but that's what we've got to do."

But then she listened to a radio news story where Governor Stitt was talking about the executive order, expressing in no uncertain terms that he wanted to send a message that he didn't want transgender people to live in the state. Lauren was enraged. She thought, "'You can drag my cold, dead corpse out of this state, personally—Kevin Stitt will have to do it himself.' I'm really motivated by spite. If the most awful thing that Governor Stitt can imagine is me and my child staying here and thriving, then we are going to do that."

The second thing that changed her mind is that aside from these political attacks, she likes Oklahoma, where Lauren has lived her entire life. "My family's lived here for such a long time—why am I the one that has to leave? I'm not the one who sucks," she states.

While there are a lot of challenges in Oklahoma—the parts that people in other parts of the country think of when they imagine the "big red belt buckle of the Bible Belt"—Lauren explains that "there are parts of it that are not bad. And there are people in it that are not bad. There's this whole community here that vehemently rejects everything that comes out of the state legislature right now. I'm optimistic enough that I want to give it a chance to change . . . which may be really stupid."

Lauren points to the change that she's seen in her own family, partly in response to their relationship with and love for Lydia: "She's changed my family's lives, just by being herself. If just her existing and thriving here can change people, then that means change is possible. And I want to give people a chance."

•

"There are endless reasons to not want to move," says Danielle, the mother of a fifteen-year-old boy named Peter and a younger child in Texas. "You want me to put a list together for you? Baby, I'll put together a list. Moving would mean taking away the first time that my kids ever had friends, the first time that they have ever felt stable in school. When they were little, Peter and his brother bounced around to a few different schools, and each time it took away their footing. I promised them that we wouldn't take that away again. We'd lose everything we built by moving—all because of a stupid law."

Part of that stability stemmed from Peter's medical transition. He has been in and out of the hospital since he was a child because of a range of medical needs, and he started having appointments with the endocrinology department at Dell Children's in Austin at the age of ten. He preempted puberty with a blocker, and at thirteen he was able to begin testosterone. Once he started transitioning, he began to settle into himself.

Danielle was devastated when her provider told her they

needed to stop seeing Peter back in May 2023. The Texas attorney general had opened an investigation into Dell Children's Medical Group Adolescent Medicine in an attempt to determine if the clinic was providing transition-related care to minors. In response, all the staff from the clinic almost immediately departed; it's unclear whether they resigned or if they were fired.[5] "We literally had our care ripped away from us," Danielle says. "And we had this absolute and utter panic. My immediate fear was that my son was going to detransition." She reached out to anyone she could think of—local LGBTQ+ youth organizations, the Austin PFLAG chapter, and the Kind Clinic. "They were all inundated with desperate parents who had just gotten a call saying that they no longer had access to care."

The situation got even worse when the Texas legislature passed the statewide healthcare ban, which also had a clause prohibiting state insurance from covering gender-affirming care for transgender youth. Peter is insured through the state; even if Danielle could find a provider in Texas to transfer his care to, they wouldn't be able to pay for it as of September 2023 when the ban took effect. "That part of the law just felt so targeted to low-income people like us," Danielle says. "They knew that these folks who had no resources would be fucked."

She began to call clinics outside of Texas but kept hearing that wait lists were stretching for nearly a year. Eventually, one of the nurses at the clinics that she called recommended a provider in Mexico—which at the time just felt daunting and maybe even dangerous. "We were literally willing to risk anything to allow him to be able to stay the way he is," Danielle shares.

She ultimately received a grant from the Campaign for Southern Equality's Southern Trans Youth Emergency Project for travel expenses, and CSE staff helped link Danielle to Elevated Access, an organization that connects patients seeking gender-affirming care to air travel, often through rides with volunteer pilots. In October 2023, she and Peter flew to Monterrey, Mexico. In a strange twist of fate, one of Danielle's childhood friends lived in the city—so he offered to be their local guide, translating Spanish and helping the family out. "It was a beautiful city, and nothing bad happened, and it ended up being an awesome trip," Danielle remembers. "The doctor was so nice and kind; she took really good care of Peter." It was a thirty-six-hour trip, but Danielle was thrilled that Peter was able to get the care he needed.

They'd love to remain under the doctor's care in Monterrey, but Danielle worries about expenses. "Every one of these trips is a minimum of $2,000," she says. "The medication, the bloodwork, the hotel—it just adds up." Peter is fifteen and thinking about the cost of at least four more trips feels untenable. But for now, Danielle and Peter are grateful for the support they have received and are trying to trust that things will work out. "The relief that we felt when we finished with our appointment was just unparalleled," Danielle says. "Both of us felt like we could breathe—and for the first time since the ban passed, we felt hope."

•

The anti-trans healthcare bans are uniquely cruel in that they take away access to something that all the families we spoke to identified as critical to their children's health and well-being.

"I think the best way to describe it is that I got to watch Lydia become herself," Lauren Green says through tears. Lydia was in foster care for a while and wasn't really listened to about her preferences or what she wanted—and particularly, how she presented herself was very policed. Lauren didn't know much about trans people or the trans community prior to adopting Lydia, but she knew that she wanted to support and affirm this young person who was expressing who she was and is. "There was a delight from her in such small things," Lauren says—things like doing her nails, or dyeing her hair purple.

Lydia turns eighteen in June 2024. And while Lauren is sad thinking about the future, when Lydia will likely move away from Oklahoma, she feels honored and proud to have supported her and helped her blossom. "To have fought so hard to get her into care—it's a long process—and people don't understand the amount of time that this takes," she says. "And now, she's just herself. . . . It was like watching her release a weight that was on her all the time, and to watch her come out of that has been really amazing."

Mike and Becca Robinson share that sense of pride about Jaxon. "We have not created any burdens for him where he feels like he cannot be himself," Mike says. "If we had been less open-minded as parents, we would have been putting limitations on and sort of tampering with his ability to continue to grow. And what a crime that would have been because I can see him being anything he wants to be. And he has the ambition to do it. So that's another reason why we just cannot live in Texas anymore. We don't want to live somewhere where there are these limitations. I'm not staying anywhere where there's a threat to my ability to raise my child."

Mike and Becca speak with wide-eyed awe about Jaxon; they gush about his status as a black belt, the way that teachers fall in love with him, the way that he excels as a percussionist and at his school subjects. "He's a borderline genius," Mike shares proudly. "And whatever he's into, he's into 100 percent. He's into being the best at everything he does."

Mike also knows that Jaxon has had an impact on the community around him, opening up the hearts and minds of his peers, their parents, and others who meet him. "People who are not inclined to grasp what being trans means, they understand it so much better now—just because they've met Jaxon. So not only does he thrive, but we get to watch other people grow as a result of being connected with him."

That's the primary source of comfort and solace for Becca

and Mike as they've navigated this turbulent, stressful period: that everything they're doing is to support their family. "We can have 100 percent confidence that we have done—and are continuing to do—the right thing because Jaxon is thriving so much," Mike says. "This can't be wrong—because this kid is so amazing."

Chapter Two

Gender-affirming care is made up of many different elements, all of which are designed to help transgender people align their physical, biological, interpersonal, and emotional traits with their gender identity. Types of care include psychotherapy, speech therapy, hormone replacement therapy, gender-affirming surgeries, and more.[1]

When Dr. Izzy Lowell launched QMed—which specializes in hormone therapy—in Atlanta, Georgia, in 2017, she figured she would be out of business within five years. "Transgender medicine is so easy—it's simple medicine. You're just replacing a hormone that somebody doesn't have," Izzy explains. "I thought this would become mundane, ubiquitous in five years or so. Everybody would be doing it."

In the meantime, Izzy planned to provide gender-affirming care to trans and gender nonconforming individuals across the South. And so, three years before telehealth went mainstream during the COVID-19 pandemic, Izzy dreamed up a revolutionary healthcare model: a practice focused on LGBTQ+ communities that would be almost 100 percent remote.

At the time, Izzy saw a growing desire among physicians to provide culturally competent care for transgender people: it wouldn't be long, she figured, before trans folks would be able to get the care they needed from their own local family physicians. And then, when it was time, she would move on to her next venture—knowing that she had helped move the needle forward on transgender healthcare.

"Obviously, I could not have been more wrong," Izzy says.

Izzy was working at Emory University Hospital in Atlanta when she thought of the idea that would eventually become QMed. She had become interested in queer and trans healthcare in medical school, seeking out resources and education on her own to learn how to provide the best care possible. Equipped with her skills and experiences, Izzy helped Emory launch a gender clinic in 2015. Initially, there was limited institutional support—and doubts that there were enough trans people in Atlanta to make the clinic viable.

But Izzy was determined to make the project work. At first, the clinic was open every other week, and patients trickled in. Yet as word got out, demand for their services grew. One afternoon, Izzy was preparing for her next appointment. She was about to go on her lunch break, and the patient was fifteen minutes late. Izzy sighed. If the patient showed up, it would throw off her whole schedule. She felt her jaw muscles tighten.

Moments later, Izzy was notified of the patient's arrival. She took a deep breath and went to meet them. The patient immediately launched into an apology: They had driven almost six hours from Tennessee and had hit bad traffic during the last part of their drive.

Izzy raised her eyebrows. And then she smiled. "Well, let's get you taken care of," she told the patient.

After that encounter, Izzy couldn't stop thinking about the distances—literal and figurative—that trans people had to go to in order to access care. It was a multi-pronged struggle: they had to find doctors who treated them like human beings, who they didn't have to educate, and who understood their bodies and used their chosen names and pronouns. In the South, in particular, such practices were scarce.

In 2019, the Campaign for Southern Equality conducted the Southern LGBTQ Health Survey, which, with more than 5,600 respondents, is the largest known survey to focus on LGBTQ+ health in the South.[2] The disparities found through this survey were startling: Nearly 40 percent of trans respondents rated their physical health as fair or poor, compared to 26 percent of cisgender respondents. At the same time, nearly half (46.8 percent) of transgender respondents rated their overall medical care as fair (35.9 percent) or poor (10.9 percent), and almost 27 percent reported that they rarely or never felt comfortable seeking care. Additionally, 57 percent of LGBTQ+ respondents said they had to educate providers about their healthcare needs.[3]

Trans southerners are not alone in having subpar health care. According to the 2015 US Transgender Survey, 19 percent of transgender respondents nationwide said they had been refused medical care due to their gender identity; 28 percent reported not seeing a doctor when they needed to because of fear of being mistreated as a transgender person; and 50 percent reported having to teach their providers about transgender healthcare.[4]

Izzy wondered why affirming healthcare should only be accessible to trans people who could leave their hometowns and drive across state lines to get it. *What if*, she thought, *trans people could get access to care where they lived?*

Enter QMed. The telehealth provider started with just a handful of patients from Georgia but quickly grew. At first, Izzy rented a small office to provide in-person care (especially since some laws required patients to meet in-person with a doctor to begin or continue hormone replacement therapy). Her team held a pop-up clinic at a camp for trans and gender nonconforming southerners in north Georgia and spread the word about their services through social media. Soon, Izzy was licensed in nearby Southern states, and steadily, she expanded QMed's reach and scope. By early 2020, QMed served more than 1,000 patients. The clinic had a dedicated office in the historic Blair Building in Decatur, Georgia, and through both virtual and in-person care, Izzy and her team served trans and gender nonconforming patients in Georgia, Florida, Kentucky, Maine, Mississippi, Virginia, and West Virginia.

Izzy was proud of her work, which she called "lifesaving" and "life-changing." Patients frequently told her and her team the impact they'd had on them—from a trans woman being less afraid to go to the doctor to trans youth feeling hopeful and joyful again. "Every day people say, 'You saved my life. I would be dead without this.' Or 'My son would be dead,'" Izzy shares. Working with trans and nonbinary patients is "just the most wonderful, happy, fulfilling thing you can do in medicine."

•

Almost ten years before Izzy started QMed, Dr. Jennifer Abbott became one of the leading transgender healthcare providers in the South by accident. "It was really just one patient," she recalls.

Jennifer is a family physician who has worked at a clinic in Western North Carolina since 2005. A few years after joining the clinic, a therapist told her about Max,[5] a transgender patient who needed a prescription for testosterone. Jennifer hesitated. "I've never done that," she told the therapist. "And I don't know *how* to do that." The therapist listened to all of Jennifer's reservations. Then, he said, "Can you just meet him?"

The therapist returned with a giant stack of papers that the patient had given him. They were printouts of the World Professional Association for Transgender Health (WPATH) standards of care for transgender patients. Jennifer hadn't learned anything about transgender health in medical school or during her residency. And she didn't quite see how it fit into family medicine. Still, she read the documents because she wanted to do right by her patients.

When Max walked into the room on the day of his appointment, Jennifer quickly learned that he had already taken many of the difficult steps on his own. He had gone to therapy, had socially transitioned, was living in the world as a man, and had come to a place of acceptance with his family. "He had already done all this hard work," Jennifer says. "The only thing he needed was a doctor to write a prescription for testosterone." Jennifer took a leap of faith and helped Max get the medicine he needed.

As the months went by, Jennifer saw Max's heart lift. "He was so happy," she says. "It was so easy, and it just made such a profound, positive impact on this person's life."

From there, word spread that Jennifer's clinic was a place where trans people in Western North Carolina could get gender-affirming care from physicians who cared about them. In that region, this was hard to come by. Every day, Jennifer heard stories from patients about going to doctor after doctor and being denied care. Some doctors said they didn't know how to treat trans patients. Others simply refused.

Jennifer and her colleagues launched a transgender health clinic in the late 2000s. By 2019, the clinic had more than 450 transgender patients. As part of this, Jennifer ran a trans teen clinic for two half-days per month. Often, a teen would arrive at her office who had been hospitalized for suicidality and was barely getting by. The parents had done everything they could think of, including trying different doctors and medications, to no avail. Jennifer would listen to the teen's and parents' stories and then educate them and share resources. She also might talk with them about gender dysphoria and link the family to a therapist who could support their child. And, if appropriate, she might initiate hormone therapy.

Jennifer repeatedly watched transgender youth with appropriate care move from surviving to thriving. Teens who were supported in their transition joined sports teams, started participating in class, and overall had better mental health outcomes. Jennifer's observations are matched by the research: studies have shown that age-appropriate gender-affirming care for transgender youth can reduce depression and anxiety, decrease suicidality, and improve body image—in both the short and long term.[6,7,8]

"It's just an amazing transformation," Jennifer says.

•

Like Jennifer, Izzy didn't intend to become an advocate for trans people and LGBTQ+ youth. She simply saw a need in the community—a community she loved—and came up with a solution.

As both a physician and a queer and gender nonconforming person, Izzy had watched the forward movement that had been occurring in trans healthcare, including a growing awareness of the transgender community by many clinicians; providers being educated by major healthcare organizations on increasing accessibility for LGBTQ+ people; and the slow advance of LGBTQ+ health into medical school curricula. Sure, it wasn't perfect—but it was a far cry from where things stood when Izzy started medical school.

Then, things shifted. In 2021, Arkansas passed a ban on gender-affirming care for minors—the first of its kind in the United States. It advanced through the legislature and was vetoed by then Republican Governor Asa Hutchinson. His veto was quickly overridden by a vote in the state legislature—but within days, a legal case had been filed challenging the law, and the courts put a halt to the ban before it took effect.[9] Over the next two years, the law remained on hold, and in 2023 a federal judge, following a trial, declared it unconstitutional.[10] (Arkansas' attorney general has appealed the ruling.[11])

After that, the flood gates opened, and state legislatures across the country proposed restrictions and bans on gender-affirming care for youth—and sometimes adults. By the end of 2023, twenty-two states had enacted laws that limited or prohibited gender-affirming care for youth—including Georgia, QMed's home, and many other states where QMed practices.[12] The laws varied in terms of target and reach. Many went after healthcare providers, while others focused on parents or children themselves. Some carried felony charges and imprisonment. Still others opened the door for civil liability.[13]

Since QMed's services originated in the South, most of its 5,000 patients (20 percent of whom are under the age of eighteen) come from states with gender-affirming care bans for youth. Patients are losing access to care, and some—especially those who can't afford to travel out of state—are being forced to go without the vital medical services they need. "It's devastating," Izzy remarks.

However, Izzy and the QMed team have found new and creative ways to continue providing care to trans youth and adults impacted by these bans. Once, Izzy took a call from a trans patient who was on a layover in Boston, Massachusetts, where providing and receiving care was still legal. Another time, she had a session with someone in a country store parking lot in Alabama, just over the state line from Mississippi, where a ban had passed into law.[14] (This was before Alabama's own gender-affirming care ban went into effect in early 2024.[15]) "We just are getting as creative as we can, but it's really hard to figure out where somebody can travel, when, getting them booked with a provider that covers that state," Izzy says. Multiply that by 1,000, and "it's my whole job."

•

The rollback of access to gender-affirming care is actually a relatively new phenomenon. Up until the past few years, the trajectory was moving in the other direction—toward expanding options, improving provider education, and ensuring that doctors were competent and skilled in supporting transgender patients. "When I was first starting in this work, we had two providers who I would have said, 'It's safe for you as a trans person to go here'—much less that they take your insurance and do informed consent," says Oliver Hall, who directs the Kentucky Health Justice Network's Trans Health Program. "And we didn't have any providers in the state doing gender-affirming surgery at the time. It's expanded considerably since."

In many ways, the late 2010s marked a historical peak in terms of access to gender-affirming care. Allison Scott, Director of Impact and Innovation for the Campaign for Southern Equality, noted that the number of affirming providers in the organization's *Trans in the South Guide* ballooned from the first edition in 2016 to the 2021 edition, which featured 400+ providers across thirteen states. "We sort of had a honeymoon period," Allison says. "It was like all of these major medical associations said, 'Trans people are real, and like many people, they need certain kinds of care, and here's an outline on how to do that.' And that's really what we saw over the past decade: the medical community embracing these medical recommendations and the science that makes a difference in our lives." (Gender-affirming healthcare for youth is supported by both decades of research and almost every major medical organization in the United States.[16, 17])

Allison remembers her own experience coming out as a trans woman and feeling like there were no good healthcare options, even in a mid-sized, progressive city like Asheville, North Carolina. "Finding care was so difficult," she recalls. "You couldn't just Google it." But things certainly expanded over time: "Providers were seeking out how to be trained and better informed on how to provide care. We had more doctors providing gender-affirming care, and that didn't lead to more people being trans—it was just addressing a need that was already there."

Oliver is grateful for the increased competency among providers—but they understand that the road to progress is often filled with stumbles. "There's a dual-sidedness of increased visibility on the whole," they say. "Unfortunately, sometimes I think we as trans people were getting some benefits from being less visible—we were only visible to the people who cared. Some of the administrative changes that we have in Kentucky—things like getting your gender marker changed—there were ways that you could work around the system because people didn't know anything about trans people. Now they're like, 'Are you trans? Are you lying to me? Do you have every document you need?'"

•

In August 2023, North Carolina became the twenty-second state to enact a gender-affirming care ban. The law prohibits the initiation of gender-affirming care in the state for people under the age of eighteen, including the use of puberty blockers, gender-affirming hormone therapy, and surgery. (It does not restrict care that has already been started.) "In my career, I've never had legislation enacted that impacted my practice of medicine," Jennifer Abbott says. She notes that doctors practice medicine using their training and scientific evidence. They also have to complete a certain number of hours of continuing education every year to maintain their licenses, skill sets, and knowledge base. "It's never really entered my practice that, okay, a bill was passed, and now I can't do the care that I know is appropriate and evidence-based."

In 2023, Jennifer went to White Coat Wednesday, an advocacy day at the North Carolina state capitol, with other physicians from the Western Carolina Medical Society. She brought with her letters from trans teen patients and their families that talked about the positive impact that gender-affirming care had had on them. She had her white coat on, and she told the lawmakers present that, "I'm a family doctor. I do gender-affirming care for teens and youth. And maybe you've never met any doctor who actually does this." She wanted to show everyone that she was a real person and "not a monster."

Jennifer also shared stories about parents who traveled from far away to find the right care for their child. "Please help my child . . . . We've tried all these other things, and they're not working," many of these parents would say to her.

"They seemed to listen," Jennifer says about the legislators who were present. But it didn't make any difference. "The vote went just completely along party lines. So it doesn't really seem to be about what an individual family needs."

•

In a health clinic in Virginia, J Gallienne, MSW, manages gender-affirming care services for a program that serves about 4,000 trans and gender nonconforming youth and adults (ages sixteen and older). A proud queer and nonbinary Appalachian, J has led multiple trans healthcare programs in the South for more than seven years.

As of February 2024, when we spoke with J, Virginia was one of only two southern states without a gender-affirming care ban. Even so, J says that many trans youth and adults in their state are afraid of losing care. Some feel an urgency to start hormone replacement therapy because they don't know what laws against it might pass tomorrow.

As more and more gender-affirming bans become law, demand for the clinic's services keeps rising. The clinic has seen an influx of trans teens and their parents who started coming to

Virginia after North Carolina's gender-affirming care ban went into effect in 2023. J also has new patients who have moved to Virginia from states with bans so they could receive care. "People don't often understand what it's like to provide this care and then also be a member of the community," J shares. J often wonders what will happen if Virginia becomes the next Florida or North Carolina. When they get overwhelmed by it all, they think of the individual conversations they've had with trans patients and families, and they remember that "this is life-saving medication and work."

Even though the work can be exhausting, J and their team find hope and joy in the ways LGBTQ+ communities—and their allies—are taking care of each other. J told us about a listserv they're on where, as bans passed, doctors started sharing resources about how and where they could legally help trans youth access care. They offered another example: J is from West Virginia, and when the state legislature was poised to pass a ban on gender-affirming care in 2023, what struck them were photos they saw of the capitol building—it was full of more than 100 protesters chanting and holding signs with messages like "I Want to See Trans Kids Become Trans Adults."[18] "There's so many people that believe in health care for *all* of us," J says.

In a follow-up email, J explains that through their work, they want "to challenge the narrative . . . that queer and trans people don't exist or belong in the South" and to continue "build[ing] support and networks in areas where there are very limited resources so that folks don't feel like they have to leave."

•

In North Carolina, Jennifer Abbott continues to legally provide care for minors who initiated care before the ban took effect—including those from neighboring states who came to her clinic due to bans in their own states. "Back when I started this care, it seemed easier," Jennifer says, even though guidelines were difficult to access and research was more limited. "Now it seems harder because of politics."

She's not giving up hope, though. In early 2024, she gave a talk to a group of medical students on providing trans- and queer-affirming care. Afterward, one of the students told her that he wanted to be a rural family physician and that he was excited about providing affirming care—but he didn't want to put off conservative people in the community.

Jennifer talked him through the subtle and structural ways he could show his support for LGBTQ+ patients. But she also reminded him that while non-LGBTQ+ people could find other places to go, his might be the only practice where LGBTQ+ people would feel safe. "You shouldn't shy away from creating that," she told him, "because these are the folks who really need that care."

Though the political situation seems bleak, "just knowing

that there's that one medical student who is imagining an affirming practice in a rural area," Jennifer says, "is really motivating."

•

In October 2023, Izzy got a call from the police. Someone had started a fire in the QMed office in Atlanta late in the night. Hate speech was also spray-painted across the side of the building. Izzy checked in with her staff after the office was vandalized, telling them they could take a step back if they needed to. Their response, according to Izzy, was, "Hell no." (The fire is being investigated as a hate crime; the QMed office in Atlanta remained closed when we spoke to Izzy in January 2024.)

Most of Izzy's time now is spent navigating the ever-changing legal landscape, talking with lawyers, and strategizing about how to keep legally providing care for her clients.

Once, she had questions about the morals of it all: As a provider, it was against her code of ethics to abandon a client without care—in other words, to end care with them if it was still needed and not help them find it elsewhere. In a 2021 interview, she talked at length about the bind these anti-trans laws were putting her in as a provider, especially the ones that forbade her from providing out-of-state resources to her patients.[19]

But that was almost three years ago. Today, "it's so far beyond ethics," she says. According to Izzy, gender-affirming care bans are both "incorrect and harmful"—and not based on medical best practices. "It's just so far over the line—for political gain—it's outrageous."

So, like Jennifer, J, and the staff at their respective clinics, Izzy and the QMed team press on. As of early 2024, QMed was serving forty-six states (with plans to expand to all fifty), and as state laws change, they are ready to provide care whenever—and wherever—it is needed.

Chapter Three

At first, many advocates for LGBTQ+ equality were convinced that the anti-transgender healthcare bans being proposed across the South were not going to pass. Sure, lawmakers might use these types of bills to campaign on or to prove their conservative bona fides, but in the end, many believed that the bills would go nowhere. Part of this disbelief stemmed from the fact that the bills were so extreme and were introduced seemingly out of the blue: banning transgender youth from accessing healthcare was simply not something the conservative movement was publicly talking about prior to 2020.

That's certainly how Katie, a resident of Mississippi, and her sixteen-year-old son, Ray, felt. The two of them first heard about potential bills restricting access to health care for trans youth at an LGBTQ+ community event in Jackson. One advocate, sensing that the tide had shifted following the US Supreme Court's *Dobbs v. Jackson Women's Health* ruling that overturned *Roe v. Wade* in 2022, told them that it was a real worry—that the far right was "coming for y'all next." "We were like, no way, no they're not," Ray says. "These bills always crop up—but the advocacy groups always get rid of them."

Members of the LGBTQ+ community had gotten used to major changes to the status quo moving slowly through the court system. In 2013 and 2014, for example, when dozens of courts ruled that bans on marriage for same-gender couples were unconstitutional, nearly all the rulings were quickly or even immediately "stayed" by the courts, meaning they would not take effect, in anticipation of appeals. Surely, many assumed, the proposed trans healthcare bans, even if they passed, would be put on hold, too, since they amounted to a major disruption of patients' medical care, and it would be judicially irresponsible to allow them to take effect. That calculus changed with the *Dobbs* ruling. Suddenly, it became evident that significant changes to Americans' basic freedoms could happen overnight.

In the months that followed *Dobbs*, a narrower type of anti-trans healthcare ban began to take hold. In South Carolina, the legislature passed a budget proviso specifically targeting the Medical University of South Carolina (MUSC) and threatening the institution's state funding if it continued providing gender-affirming care to transgender people under the age of sixteen.[1] In response, MUSC almost immediately stopped providing care to *all* transgender minors (even those who were sixteen and seventeen years old), forcing hundreds of families to seek care elsewhere in the state.

This overcompliance has been present everywhere. In Texas, political pressure led to the closure of Genecis, a specialty clinic for transgender adolescents based at Children's Medical Center in Dallas.[2] In Mississippi, the TEAM Clinic (an acronym for Trustworthy, Evidence-Based, Affirming, and Multidisciplinary) at the University of Mississippi Medical Center (UMMC) buckled to intense political pressure as well, abruptly ceasing the provision of gender-affirming care to minors in the fall of 2022. This seemed to be an attempt to appease the state legislature and preempt lawmakers from shutting down the clinic entirely before the implementation of House Bill 1125 (HB 1125), known as the Regulate Experimental Adolescent Procedures Act, which would ban transgender care for minors in the state.[3]

Ray was a patient at UMMC when his dad received a phone call telling him that the clinic would no longer be able to see his son. They didn't explain why. Ray loved the doctor that he had been seeing for nearly a year—but now he and his family had to scramble for care.

•

Jensen Matar runs an organization in Mississippi called the T.R.A.N.S. Program. Jensen, who is transgender, has been organizing around transgender and queer issues in the state for nearly a decade. His journey began in the early 2010s when he had to advocate for himself due to rampant anti-transgender hostility while working at a department store. That experience lit a fuse, and he began volunteering with the ACLU of Mississippi in 2016, contributing to their Transgender Education and Advocacy Program (TEAP), the first-ever program solely dedicated to transgender people in the state. Alongside his friend Malaysia Walker, a transgender woman who served as the first coordinator of the program, Jensen helped develop resources for transgender Mississippians, build coalitions, educate trans people about their rights, and share information with the broader community, lawmakers, and law enforcement. Jensen ultimately became the full-time coordinator of TEAP.

In 2017, Jensen wrote an op-ed for Mississippi's largest newspaper, *The Clarion-Ledger*, which was the first-ever piece by an out transgender person published by the paper. "I am valuable as you are valuable," he wrote. "All transgender and gender nonconforming people are valuable. We are civil, hardworking members of society with dreams and aspirations. We deserve to be seen, heard, protected, and treated as equal. We live here in Mississippi. I am Mississippi. We are ALL Mississippi. And we belong here."[4]

Funding for TEAP dried up in 2020 as the COVID-19 pandemic raged across the country, but Jensen and other trans leaders in the state knew that they couldn't let the services and resources they had built up dissipate. "Mississippi had nothing when it came to resources for trans folks," Jensen says. "We thought, 'Who's going to educate? Who's going to speak out for us?'"

Jensen worked with his colleagues to start a new project—the T.R.A.N.S. Program (Transgender Resources, Advocacy, Networking, and Services). While it was initially geared toward adult transgender people, as well as supporting cisgender parents as they navigated their children coming out as trans, the legislative chaos of 2022 and 2023 compelled the program to focus on blocking the dangerous anti-trans youth legislation that was being considered by lawmakers—and then supporting families impacted by the law after it was passed. For example, the organization's monthly TRANSparent support call, for parents and caregivers of trans and nonbinary youth, became distinctly focused on HB 1125. "It was really heartbreaking to be on some of these support calls with the parents, breaking down in tears, trying to figure out what they can do to make sure their family is okay," Jensen recalls. "The most vulnerable of the vulnerable were being attacked—and then on top of that, so many of these families of trans youth were already feeling overwhelmed to begin with about how to become an ally, how to identify healthcare options, how best to support their kid."

In some ways, Jensen views the work of the T.R.A.N.S. Program as a different form of practical support—tending to the tangible, emotional, social needs of trans people and their loved ones. "All we do at the T.R.A.N.S. Program is communicate with the people reaching out to us and listen to them,"

Jensen says. "You'd be surprised at how far it would go to listen to people, let them vent to you, befriend them. Relationships are so important—especially in times of high stress and in times of pain and mourning."

Jensen worked with other organizations, including the ACLU of Mississippi, Human Rights Campaign, the Spectrum Center, and Immigrant Alliance for Justice and Equity, to host a rally in Jackson to speak out against HB 1125. Dozens of community members, some with the pink, blue, and white of the transgender pride flag wrapped around their shoulders and many holding signs that said, "Protect Trans Youth," marched around the governor's mansion. Afterward, the participants formed an arc behind a podium outside of the state capitol and held a press conference to express just how harmful the bill would be.

The rally took place the day before Ray's seventeenth birthday. Katie shared a few words at the press conference. "He's always been a great kid. But he's been able to open up so much more after accessing this gender-affirming care," she said about her son. "This bill would change our lives because it would make it impossible for us to get the care that Ray needs—and that we're in the middle of right now."[5]

Ray explains the impact that gender-affirming care had on him from a young age. "It's always been very, very intense," he says of the gender dysphoria he experienced. "I had horrible anxiety tics, because my body could not contain what was happening." He would blink uncontrollably, fidget with his hands, and cough every few minutes. That all changed when he started seeing a therapist for gender dysphoria. "The tics went away when I started socially transitioning at fourteen—the physical manifestations just went away," he says. Things improved even more when he began taking a puberty blocker and later started hormone therapy. "I don't know how I would have functioned if I hadn't been allowed that medicine," Ray says. "I was so afraid of everything, and my self-confidence has rocketed since then. I was allowed to live."

"I see what it's done," Katie adds. "I see him thriving."

Press coverage poured in the night of the rally as the clock struck midnight on Ray's birthday. Articles and videos featuring sympathetic stories about the importance of transgender equality shone a light on how dismantling access to gender-affirming care could result in an increase in self-harm or suicidal ideation by young trans people in Mississippi. "I will do anything—anything—to keep my child from feeling that way," Katie told reporters.[6]

It was a positive day, lifting the spirits of advocates and attendees. And while the bill passed in the Mississippi House, it became stalled in the State Senate as lawmakers raised serious concerns. "There was a lot of hope," Katie says. "And then it was squashed."

One week later, the Senate pushed the bill to passage, and Governor Tate Reeves vowed to sign it. However, even with that looming meteor, there were no discussions of a lawsuit being filed against the ban—largely because the Fifth Circuit Court of Appeals, which represents Mississippi, is so deeply unfriendly to a wide range of issues, including those concerning the LGBTQ+ community, that a suit would have a limited chance of success.

A week before the rally, Jensen received an email from the team at the Campaign for Southern Equality—how could they help?

•

With the Mississippi ban looking increasingly likely to take effect, the Campaign for Southern Equality hopped into gear. Though based in Asheville, North Carolina, the organization had some history in Mississippi—leading lawsuits against the state's ban on marriage for same-gender couples in 2014, its ban on legal adoption for same-gender couples in 2015, and the 2016 passage of House Bill 1523, a broad law that granted business owners and others a "license to discriminate" against LGBTQ+ people.

The organization's leaders were concerned that if HB 1125 passed, there wouldn't be adequate infrastructure in place to help families of transgender youth preserve continuity of care for their children. After all, there was no blueprint for an anti-transgender healthcare bill taking effect and disrupting care.

Unlike HB 1125, most of the bans being discussed in other states at the time had effective dates several months in the future, which would provide advocates a bit more time to prepare if they did become law. "When we started game-planning what it would be like to rise to this occasion and find a workable fix for families, we realized that we had many of the fundamentals in place to lend our support," explains Allison Scott, Director of Impact and Innovation at CSE. "We needed to package the elements that we had for the specific needs of transgender youth and the specific needs of this awful legislation."

The year prior, CSE had gotten a preview of how to support southern families of transgender youth when the Texas attorney general issued an opinion that declared it "child abuse" for parents to provide gender-affirming care to their transgender children. Following this, the Texas Department of Family and Protective Services began opening investigations into families. As Equality Texas, Transgender Education Network of Texas (TENT), and legal organizations led on advocacy and legal strategies for opposing this directive, CSE opened a round of emergency grants, featuring a simple application that allowed families to access $250, which could be used to pay for a lawyer, develop safety protocols for their children, or to defray other costs. A few months later, when Alabama's anti-trans healthcare ban took effect for a week, CSE provided support to families by encouraging providers in the state to let their patients know that they were eligible for the organization's emergency grants.

The grants project was an outgrowth of the Southern Equality Fund, which provided microgrants to support organizations doing queer and trans work in the South, as well as directly to LGBTQ+ southerners during the COVID-19 pandemic. "We've been grantmaking to individuals and grassroots groups all throughout the South," Allison shares. "We had a viable grantmaking solution and were able to scale it up to grant individually to a few thousand people at a time. So we knew that we could move money in large quantities."

CSE was also able to quickly strengthen its relationships with several providers of gender-affirming care in states outside of Mississippi. Since 2016, the organization has regularly published the *Trans in the South Guide*, a directory of trans-affirming healthcare and legal service providers across the South. Community members submit the names of many of the providers, and CSE works to build the list out further. These contacts were a first step in initiating conversations with providers who could support trans Mississippians in the post-HB 1125 landscape.

Katie and Ray were one of the first families to receive support from the Campaign for Southern Equality's emerging rapid-response services. Jensen initially connected the family with CSE for a media request, but it quickly became clear that Katie needed support identifying a provider for Ray. The family—Katie, Ray, and Ray's father and stepmom—already had a long-term plan in place: Ray's father, who has had shared joint custody with Katie since the couple divorced more than a decade ago, had recently gotten a job in Northern Virginia. The plan was for Ray to spend his last two years in high school with his dad and stepmom so that he could continue his medical care without interruption. "It just felt like he had to go," Katie says. "It was extremely hard for me to admit that that was what was best for him. It's the hardest thing I've ever had to do."

However, the move was still a few months away, and Ray needed his medicine immediately. To fill in the gap, CSE connected Katie and Ray with QMed, who talked them through the process of driving across the border to get medication—at the time, the closest destination was Alabama, which was four hours away by car. Katie and Ray chronicled the story of their road trip in a powerful article in *The Washington Post*. The article closed with Ray successfully getting the medicine that would get him through to the move:

> "I feel more relieved than I have in months," [Katie] said. "I can't think of a single thing I have to worry about." She knew that relief was temporary. Soon, Ray would be gone, and she'd be left with a hole where her sweet teenage boy should be. For now, she tried to enjoy the last hour of their road trip. They talked about road kill and theater camp, boys, and a new Greek restaurant they wanted to try. Eventually, once they crossed back into Mississippi, they went quiet.[7]

•

Around the same time that HB 1125 was making its way through the Mississippi state government, a blanket ban on gender-affirming care for transgender youth was advancing rapidly through the Tennessee legislature.

In Memphis, Tyler was helping to facilitate an LGBTQ+ youth group at OUTMemphis, a local LGBTQ+ center. The group had been meeting virtually since the COVID-19 pandemic began, and Tyler was determined to bring people back together face to face. "One of my goals was to bring it back to in-person programming," Tyler says. "We really tried to get the word out that we're back—the center is open, and if you need a safe space, we are absolutely here for you. We had a small group at first, but we were really picking up momentum. And then Tennessee passed a gender-affirming care ban, and our role looked so different."

After the ban passed in March 2023, several OUTMemphis staff members, including Tyler, began regularly traveling 200 miles to the state capitol in Nashville to do advocacy work, plan rallies, and attend committee hearings. "Talking to each of our participants and their families, their needs are so highly individualized," Tyler explains. "You could put together a resource guide. You can hold town halls educating people on legislation. But when it comes down to it, the parents are their own case managers for their kids. They're the ones navigating these extremely complicated questions around insurance and coverage and what's even legal—and potentially being considered a liability to your child for helping them seek healthcare."

In 2023, OUTMemphis's youth program, PRYSM, expanded from a single support group to a collection of services for LGBTQ+ and transgender youth, including providing direct resources for families as well as case management. The organization hired a full-time staff member, Sarah, to help with the expansion and provide care navigation services to parents and families who need help steering through the labyrinthine paths to accessing care for their kids. "It's easier for us to pick up our entire lives than to deal with the constant bombardment of bad news for my kid's identity," many parents tell Sarah. "Thankfully, those parents have the ability to do that, but there are so many kids who are stuck in families who don't have the means to leave—or they just don't even feel comfortable coming out to their family."

Many of the conversations Sarah has with parents are simply explaining what gender-affirming hormone therapy is—because most doctors in Tennessee refuse to see or speak to parents who want to access care for their trans kids. Sarah explains that "I had one [parent] who said, 'Oh, I tried talking to an endocrinologist about getting my kid onto hormone therapy, and they straight-up wouldn't talk to me.'"

In states like Tennessee, where civil prosecution or criminal charges are possible, many providers fear being sued or arrested for even discussing gender-affirming care with their patients.

•

By March 2023, trans youth healthcare bans were imminent in almost every southern state, and CSE realized that an overarching regional program was necessary. As a result, the organization launched the Southern Trans Youth Emergency Project (STYEP).

CSE hired two part-time staff members to serve as navigators for the project, which connected parents for one-on-one conversations about their options for continuing gender-affirming care for their child out of state. On the call, the navigator would also process a grant for $250 (which soon increased to $500), which could be used for anything the family needed; most families used the grant to pay for the increased costs of traveling to or initiating care with a new provider. "We were really inspired by the reproductive justice movement," says Carolyn Jones, one of the first navigators, who later became STYEP's program manager. "Reproductive rights organizations and abortion funds have been doing this work for a long time—since before *Roe v. Wade* was overturned—in supporting people in getting the abortions that they need when they need them. We modeled a lot of this work on that work, and we had conversations with many leaders in the abortion access space to formulate our program."

Organizations like the Brigid Alliance, which assists people who need to travel for an abortion, helped give an idea of what long-distance travel for trans healthcare might require, while Jane's Due Process, an organization that assists young people in Texas on how to navigate parental consent laws and abortion bans, provided insight into how to best support minors forced to travel for care. The abortion fund model did need to be adapted for the specifics of gender-affirming care, which requires three to four appointments per year to a provider (rather than one-time travel as in the case of an abortion.)

The CSE team didn't have to reinvent the wheel—but they did need to figure out how the wheels fit together to create an effective program for families in crisis.

•

While CSE was implementing STYEP, the state of Kentucky became embroiled with its own anti-transgender legislation. A monster bill was introduced that would censor curriculum in schools, encourage teachers and school staff to "out" transgender students to their parents, and prohibit best-practice medical care for transgender youth.[8]

Oliver Hall was ready to fight.

For six years, Oliver had been working at the Kentucky Health Justice Network (KHJN). Founded in 2008 by several women of color, KHJN operates multiple programs encompassing direct support for abortion and gender-affirming care, as well as education, for people in Kentucky. It is one of a few organizations in the country that provide tangible guidance for transgender people looking for help in understanding their healthcare options. KHJN was one of the first groups the Campaign for Southern Equality reached out to when the anti-trans law started advancing in Kentucky.

Through a 2014 community-based needs assessment in partnership with a trans research group called TSTAR (Trans and Sexuality Teaching, Advocacy, and Research), KHJN gained insight into trans Kentuckians who needed to access healthcare. As a college undergraduate, Oliver saw this research, which inspired them to pursue an internship at KHJN. During their internship, Oliver proposed a Trans Health Program to focus on direct support, education, and funding. The program became a reliable way to support transgender health care needs in the state, providing assistance on a wide range of issues and offering funding for emergency safety and security needs. Oliver now serves as the director of KHJN's Trans Health program.

Oliver's eyes were first opened to the need for collective organizing when their dad, who worked for a railroad company and was exposed to asbestos poisoning, received a settlement late in his career through his union that barely covered his medical bills. In college, Oliver organized with a group called United Students Against Sweatshops.

Oliver was also inspired by abortion funds. "An abortion fund is the perfect place to implement another direct support program for another type of stigmatized health care," they say. "We can work toward addressing people's immediate needs." Oliver's personal experience with abortion care also informs their activism. They had an abortion at nineteen, and while Oliver was not out as trans at the time, they were "visibly gender nonconforming" and felt uncomfortable going to the only place available—a women's surgical center. "I ended up self-managing my abortion, which was the right choice for me—but it felt like my only choice," Oliver shares. "I knew I wanted to get involved in reproductive justice and make sure other trans people coming behind me were not feeling the way that I was feeling."

When the trans youth healthcare ban passed in Kentucky, it didn't require much of a pivot for Oliver and the KHJN team. While they needed to increase their budget for fuel because families would have to travel further distances, the rest of their support infrastructure was already in place. "A lot of my drive comes from, even as a White middle-class trans person, having experiences that really overlapped in a specific way that people weren't addressing," Oliver explains. "There was the financial aspect of being able to access an abortion, there was the lack of provider knowledge that stopped me from accessing an in-clinic abortion. Just acknowledging that and saying, 'Hmmm, we should really try to do something about that. Let's start trying, and we'll figure it out.'"

•

By the end of the summer of 2023, nearly every state in the South had passed a healthcare ban for transgender youth, and most were in effect—from Georgia to Louisiana to Texas to North Carolina. To meet this moment, CSE expanded the Southern Trans Youth Emergency Project to thirteen states. The expansions usually began with a comprehensive canvass of state and local partners and a virtual "town hall" event. Questions were pre-submitted to the town hall by families who wanted to know how they could continue healthcare for their child or whether they risked arrest or criminal penalties by driving across state lines. Attendance at these town halls was often over 100 families.

The CSE team was also busy, fielding more than fifty requests for support per week to help with patient navigation to out-of-state health care providers and to provide emergency grants. Some of the families on these calls were extremely well-prepared and reached out prior to the bans taking effect, sometimes even before they passed. These families were usually very tuned into the news and political developments and wanted to make sure that there were absolutely no gaps in their child's care. For other families, the conversations constituted an emergency: many were caught unaware by the new laws, and were blindsided when they showed up for a long-scheduled appointment only to realize they could no longer legally access care. "For these families, it can be a real shock, learning that the law is in effect," Carolyn Jones of CSE says. "We are usually able to quell the panic and talk them through their options."

At several clinics, CSE has set up patient care funds—a pool of funding that providers are able to tap into to cover the clinical costs for families traveling from states with bans. Families who are forced to travel for health care often have to see providers who are out-of-network on their insurance coverage, which can significantly increase costs. The patient care funds are one step toward closing the gap for families who are uninsured or underinsured.

The STYEP team has also become a bit of an emergency hotline operation. Often, parents contact the team in dismay, explaining that key logistics for their trip out of state have been derailed and that they need help identifying solutions. One Texas parent, for example, had scheduled an appointment in New Mexico, lining up her family's lodging and flight—only to have the clinic abruptly cancel the appointment due to worries about newly aggressive moves from the Texas attorney general. Carolyn was able to quickly connect the parent with QMed, allowing her to keep the same flight and lodging for the visit. Other inquiries have come from families in Alabama and North Carolina, where pharmacies have refused to fill prescriptions despite the fact that they are still legally allowed to. CSE staffers have canvassed pharmacies in certain states where this "overcompliance" has occurred and passed on information to partner organizations with corporate relationships to the pharmacies, urging them to resist over-complying unnecessarily with the bans.

Other calls come from families with young children who are not yet ready to medically transition. These callers are not seeking a grant—but rather, information and reassurance that there will be help when their family is ready for the next step in their journey. "There is a clear level of emotional support that is happening on these calls," Carolyn shares. "Often these parents are not in community with parents of trans children and feel like they are on an island. They are processing the idea that their legislature, in what is often their home state, has voted against what they know to be the best way to love and support their child. So sometimes we are just there as a listening ear—answering questions, what to do next, and making sure they know how much we, as advocates, appreciate them moving mountains for their children."

Carolyn is hopeful about the trans community's response to these draconian healthcare bans. People from across the country, including from large metropolitan cities and small rural towns in every state, have stepped up with donations, fundraisers, and messages of support for transgender youth. By the summer of 2024, support for the program had become so evident—and the nationwide need so clear—that the project, now called the Trans Youth Emergency Project, was expanded to include youth from any state with a ban on gender-affirming care.

Carolyn and the CSE team often hear personal stories that illustrate the solidarity that exists even in the most surprising places: "It's very, very clear to me that these legislatures and these laws are not representative of what the people in these states want." She explains that one of the earliest families she helped with navigation and funding was from a rural part of Mississippi. Their transgender child was enrolled in a private conservative Christian middle school and was nervous about coming out—but when she did, she was met with support from the administration, fellow students, and other parents at the school. "Those are the stories that really show how the legislators are out of step with the reality of what it's like to be a community that supports each other," Carolyn says. "And if that can happen in rural Mississippi, then I believe that it *is* happening everywhere, and it can happen everywhere."

•

In the wake of the Tennessee ban, OUTMemphis has expanded its youth services, becoming more active in advocacy efforts in Memphis and across the state. Several of the organization's staff still frequently travel to Nashville to weigh in on issues related to transgender and queer youth—including a heinous bill that passed in 2024 that would put LGBTQ+ youth in harm's way by allowing non-affirming foster parents to care for them. "Nashville is known to have a much louder voice than west Tennessee when it comes to LGBTQ advocacy," Tyler explains. OUTMemphis wants to be sure that perspectives from the western part of the state are heard and considered.

Back home in Memphis, Tyler shares that the organization is doing a lot of coalition building. "A lot of the smaller orgs that primarily serve Black trans folks in Memphis are often left out of these conversations and are left out of these opportunities to go to the state capital. So for us, it's been inviting them, making sure they're on these email threads, making sure they're trained and prepared and feeling comfortable."

For both Tyler and Sarah, part of their efforts to make advocacy accessible is elevating the voices of trans youth, who, Tyler says, are "extremely overwhelmed by the attacks on their bodies and their community—and at the same time, they want to let people know how they feel about it. They have been on podcasts, they have spoken at our rallies, they've done interviews for different media outlets. . . . They want to be vocal. They want to be seen, and they want to be heard."

Oliver of KHJN has also felt inspired by the families they have served. "It's been really heartwarming to see how many parents are really, really invested in making sure their children get care," they say. "They're like, 'Hey, gas money would be helpful—but we're going to do anything we can. Like, I'll take out a second mortgage—I'm not going to let my kid not get the care they need.' I usually wind up crying after we have those calls."

Yet, there is always more to be done. "The biggest thing that we always hear is, 'Oh my god, y'all do so much,'" Tyler says. "But the thing that keeps us up at night is all the things we could still be doing more of."

•

For Ray, living in Northern Virginia has been a stark improvement, compared to living in Mississippi. "I have the most in common with international immigrants because it feels like a different country," he says of his new, temporary home. "I don't think I've ever *not* been in culture shock since moving. I always thought, 'This is normal. You're supposed to be a little bit afraid.' And then I moved to Fairfax, and I saw that's not what you're supposed to feel at all."

In terms of medical care, Ray feels like his options are now bountiful: instead of one provider in the entire state, there are four in his region alone. And he's meeting many new friends and allies. "In middle school, I could count on my hands the number of trans people I knew in the entire world," he says. "In this school, I can't even count the number of trans people in our theater program."

While Ray is starting to thrive in his new home, the move was hard at first for his mother, Katie, who missed her son a great deal. "Ray is doing really well," she shares. "And I'm still here. And I'm okay. At first, I was not okay—but I am okay now."

In the first part of 2024, Mississippi lawmakers pushed a fresh wave of anti-transgender legislation, including a bill that would prohibit transgender people from using the restroom in line with their gender identity.

But even as the Mississippi queer and trans community fought back hard against these attacks, they found ways to share joy.

March 31 marks the annual Trans Day of Visibility (TDOV)—an opportunity to celebrate and elevate the voices, experiences, and successes of transgender people. Since 2017, the community in Jackson, Mississippi, and across the state have come together for a celebratory day of visibility and action. The event in 2023 was powerful—but it also came just weeks after HB 1125 took effect, and the weight of the law loomed large over everyone. In 2024, the event felt more hopeful and resistant, with the community uniting for action, friendship, and hope.

Jensen from the T.R.A.N.S. Program explains that the park where the event is held—Fondren Park, in a "progressive little corner" of Jackson—is the only public space in Mississippi that has properly and publicly acknowledged the trans and nonbinary community in the state. The city granted permission for advocates to build and maintain a permanent planter bed and plaque in honor of the trans community. Each year, TDOV attendees plant flowers that are the colors of the trans flag. One year, an artist added steel butterfly wings to the installation to pay tribute to Dominique "DeDe" Jackson, a Black transgender woman who was killed in the city in 2021.[9]

From across the state, community organizations come together on TDOV, tabling with information and resources, while trans and nonbinary vendors are invited to sell their products or offer services like haircuts, gender-affirming clothing, and more. There's even a stage where any trans person is invited to speak, perform—or just strut their stuff. "We tried to enable any trans or nonbinary person to be visible in any way that they wanted to be visible," Jensen shares. Creating spaces like this, he says, is critical. "These kids just want to be loved and supported. Do you remember when you were sixteen or seventeen? All you want to do is feel like you belong. All you want to do is feel like you can participate and feel like you're in the right spot and that people like you. That's precisely the need, and that's precisely what these kids are increasingly told they cannot have. And now it's gone to the extreme—not only can you not have this, but we're also going to make it clear that we *don't* recognize you, we *don't* want you here, we *don't* like you. That's what our state is telling this vulnerable, tiny population."

One of the speakers at the 2024 TDOV event in Jackson was Ray, who was visiting his mom during his high school spring break. He appeared on the stage wearing aviator sunglasses and a black button-up shirt printed with blue and pink hibiscus flowers. The stage was festooned with pink, blue, and white fabric, and the podium Ray stood behind featured a sign that said, "Trans People Belong Here." Ray said into the microphone:

> I was forced to leave the state I love by hate-fueled politicians. Before I moved states, I experienced the typical 'Being Trans in Mississippi' package that I'm sure you're all very familiar with: school bullies, slurs, frustrating administrators, and a principal that called me a predator when I was five-foot-nothing and afraid of my own shadow. But I'm not here because of those people. I'm standing here today because my family has supported me and loved me, even when they didn't fully understand me. I'm here because of the T.RA.N.S. Program, the HRC Foundation, and Safe Harbor Church, all of which are spaces that have prevailed in the face of hate over and over and over again. I'm here because I've experienced so much love—and that's what I'm here to talk about. Love. For any young trans person who is listening to me right now, I need you to know a couple of things. You are loved. I know it feels like your resistance is an act of rebellion—and that's true, I won't argue with that—but you are also made of love. . . . You are needed. The world won't change without you being there to make it happen. And I need you there to make it happen.

Chapter Four

Superstar litigator Alexia Korberg never intended to become a partner at a big law firm. In fact, when they started at Yale Law School in 2009, their eyes were set on one thing and one thing only: making the world a better place for LGBTQ+ people.

To try and make that happen, Alexia interned at the American Civil Liberties Union and the New York Civil Liberties Union, where they worked on LGBTQ+ rights cases and participated in a Yale Law School clinic where they represented queer Iraqi immigrants seeking refugee status. Alexia was so confident in their professional trajectory that they sidestepped recruiting events with major law firms and even skipped classes to take the train from New Haven, Connecticut, to their unpaid internships in New York City.

During their second year of law school, Alexia had lunch with James Esseks, the director of the ACLU's LGBTQ and HIV Project. Alexia asked which of the LGBTQ+ impact litigation organizations they should go to next. James' response surprised Alexia. "He told me . . . I needed to really learn how to be a lawyer first," Alexia recalls. He encouraged them to apply to one of the big law firms in New York City—Paul, Weiss—which had an excellent training program for young lawyers. And, James added, he had it on good authority that the firm was about to file a challenge to the Defense of Marriage Act (DOMA), the federal legislation passed in 1996 that defined marriage as only between a man and a woman, barring same-gender couples from accessing the federal protections and responsibilities that marriage provided even if they were legally married in a state with the freedom to marry.[1]

Alexia followed James' advice, and soon they were working "at every level" of the *United States v. Windsor* case. The plaintiff, Edie Windsor, had been married to her spouse, Thea Spyer, for forty-four years before the latter passed in 2009. (The couple got married in Canada in 2007, and their marriage was recognized by the state of New York, where they lived.) Because of DOMA, Windsor couldn't claim the estate tax marital deduction that would've been available to her if Thea had been a man. "Edie and Thea were treated as legal strangers for tax purposes," Alexia explains. "So Edie had to pay taxes on 50 percent of everything she had accumulated with Thea over their decades-long relationship and liquidate her retirement savings to fork over hundreds of thousands of dollars to the government." In 2010, Edie filed a lawsuit against the federal government for refusing to recognize her marriage.[2] Edie's case eventually made it to the US Supreme Court, which ruled the core of DOMA to be unconstitutional in 2013. This landmark decision helped pave the way for the freedom to marry for all couples in the United States.

Building off this huge win, a few years later, Alexia and their colleagues successfully litigated a series of pro bono cases in Mississippi that invalidated the state's bans on marriage for same-gender couples and adoption by LGBTQ+ families.

"For a while, I only won," they said, laughing. "I'm on a losing streak lately."

•

As we have seen, in the last few years, waves of legal and policy attacks targeting the LGBTQ+ community have swept across the US. As noted in the introduction to this book, in 2023 alone, the ACLU tracked 510 anti-LGBTQ+ bills that were proposed in forty-eight states, eighty-four of which were passed into law.[3] From 2021 to the sumer of 2024, twenty-five states enacted laws limiting youth access to gender-affirming care—and almost all are facing legal challenges.[4]

Among these suits is Alexia's most recent pro bono case, *Poe v. Labrador*, which they filed in 2023 with the ACLU, the ACLU of Idaho, W/rest Collective, and Groombridge, Wu, Baughman, and Stone LLP as co-counsels. In this case, two families in Idaho assert that House Bill 71 (HB 71)—a gender-affirming care ban for minors that was signed into law by Governor Brad Little in May 2023—violates the constitutional rights of transgender youth and their parents.[5]

The case came on the heels of another case that Alexia worked on between 2018 and 2022, the earth-shaking *Dobbs v. Jackson Women's Health Organization*, in which they represented Mississippi's last abortion clinic.

When Alexia heard that Idaho was poised to pass a criminal ban on gender-affirming care for minors, they initially hesitated to step into the fray again—for multiple reasons. The *Windsor* case had been one of Alexia's first lawsuits. While they were not the only queer lawyer working on the case, Alexia was often the only "*visibly* queer" person in the room. They remembered sitting at a deposition table and listening as opposing lawyers suggested that LGBTQ+ people—people like Alexia—were a danger to children. At another deposition, the opposition used the derogatory notion of "lesbian until graduation" (i.e., the idea that some women experiment with same-gender relationships in college but marry men after graduation) to try and prove that queerness is a mutable trait (rather than recognizing the validity of bisexuality or pansexuality).

Alexia came out publicly as transgender in 2021, and they were not eager to be under the microscope again, especially as a transgender lawyer litigating a case in support of transgender rights. To be a lawyer, they explained, you have to "crawl inside the other side's argument," accept it, and then figure out "how to crawl out." In other words, one has to immerse oneself in the opposition's argument and ideals, acknowledge them as potentially valid, and then counter with an opposing argument. In this case, Alexia had to crawl inside the argument that, as a trans person, "you don't exist."

"Day-to-day existence as a trans person right now is just so demoralizing," they share. "Having to litigate my very existence and dignity is draining and difficult in a way that I couldn't have fully predicted."

•

In part, Alexia traces the uptick in anti-trans laws back to September 2021, when the Supreme Court let Senate Bill 8 (SB 8) go into effect in Texas. "That moment changed the course of American history, and it changed LGBTQ+ rights," they say. SB 8 banned abortions as early as five weeks after the start of a patient's last menstrual cycle (before many people even know they are pregnant). It also supported "vigilante anti-abortion enforcement," meaning that, as Alexia says, "regular people were empowered to go after anyone they suspected of having had an abortion."[6] Alexia calls the law "bananas unconstitutional." At the time, *Roe v. Wade* was still the law of the land, and it was unconstitutional to ban abortion prior to twenty-three weeks. Alexia says that when the Supreme Court allowed SB 8 to remain in place, "it emboldened legislators in states all over the place to start passing blatantly unconstitutional laws under the belief that maybe this Supreme Court will allow them to go into effect." Alexia also believes that "the connections between anti-abortion laws, anti-LGBTQ laws, assaults on bodily autonomy—and anything that's a threat to patriarchy—run very deep" and that all these laws are lifted from the same playbook.

Alexia first came out publicly as trans in an op-ed in *The Washington Post* where they drew a link between SB 8 and an anti-LGBTQ+ law passed in Mississippi several years earlier:

> Mississippi passed a prototype for the Texas law [in 2016]—a sweeping anti-LGBTQ law titled the Religious Liberty Accommodations Act that gives the public license to target gay and trans people for discrimination, and the right to sue and collect money from anyone who tries to interfere. The text of Mississippi's law offers multiple pages of the types of discrimination it invites: Landlords can evict gay and trans renters. Businesses can refuse service to LGBTQ people. Doctors and nurses can decline to treat LGBTQ people.... The law also permits and protects "expressive conduct"—vitriol and harassment.[7]

The Campaign for Southern Equality was the plaintiff in a lawsuit challenging the Mississippi law, and Alexia was one of the lawyers who litigated the case. Ultimately, though, the law went into effect in 2018—and the US Supreme Court refused to hear the appeal.

According to Alexia, laws like the Religious Liberty Accommodations Act and SB 8 have "emboldened and ushered in this totally unprecedented regime of laws that have the designed purpose and effect of terrorizing people."

•

Certainly, many LGBTQ+ people—especially transgender people—are living in fear these days. Across multiple states, age groups, and situations, one of the predominant words we heard when interviewing people for this book was "fear."

There are many different types of fear. Doctors are afraid to provide gender-affirming care for their trans patients. Trans youth and their parents in so-called "safe" states fear that their legislature will be the next one to pass a gender-affirming care ban. Black and Brown trans folks fear harassment and discrimination in workplaces, stores, and bathrooms—along with being scared of violent encounters with police. Trans students fear being bullied—by other students and by school staff. Providers and community organizations fear—and have experienced—vandalism and violent hate crimes.

One of the reasons for this fear is that, unlike the anti-LGBTQ+ legislation discussed in the 2010s, more recently passed legislation is firmer, more sweeping, and less hypothetical. This legislation is not like "license to discriminate" laws or even nondiscrimination laws that technically empower someone to discriminate or technically protect them if they are the victim of discrimination. That is, some types of anti-LGBTQ+ bills seem more about trying to create a climate of harassment, especially since enforcement of such laws can be so selective.

But recently, anti-transgender laws have literally changed the landscape of what a trans person can and cannot do. From healthcare bans to bans on athletic participation, these policies are like cruel light switches—taking something that was once possible and immediately switching it off.

In 2022, we saw Texas attempt its own kind of "light switch" when Attorney General Ken Paxton issued a memo declaring that parents helping their transgender children access gender-affirming care "can legally constitute child abuse."[8] The nonbinding memo directed the Texas Department of Family Protective Services (DFPS) to investigate parents of transgender young people. The response was almost immediate, as nearly a dozen families reported being investigated by DFPS in the days following the memo's release. The parents were shocked by the potential consequences: just for affirming their transgender child, they could be declared unfit parents, and their children could be taken away from them.

Amber and Adam Briggle were one of the first families to receive a call from DFPS. They live in North Texas and have long been outspoken supporters of their teenage son Grayson, who is transgender, and their entire family, including their youngest child Mae.

When Amber first got the message from DFPS, she burst into tears. The DFPS investigator told her that she was on her way to the family's home. Amber asked that she come to her office instead, and the investigator agreed. At the office, the investigator informed the family that they had been reported for engaging with their son's "transgender transformation." She confirmed that she was investigating because of Paxton's memo and that she'd have to search the Briggles' home.

Amber and Adam were forced to quickly hire an attorney to represent themselves and an additional attorney to represent Grayson and their other child, Mae. When the home investigation occurred a few days later, the investigator opened every drawer and cabinet in the house, inspected food and other items in the kitchen and bathrooms, interviewed Amber and Adam, and then, separately, interviewed nine-year-old Mae and fourteen-year-old Grayson. She also asked the Briggles to authorize a release of Grayson's medical records, which they refused. "I have never felt more invaded in the place that I feel the safest—ever," Adam wrote later in an evidentiary declaration for a legal challenge to the attorney general's directive.[9] "I observed how [my family] looked uncomfortable, anxious, and even scared as their home was invaded . . ."

This was not the first time that Amber and Adam had to

defend themselves against claims that they were committing "child abuse." In 2021 Amber testified against Senate Bill 1646, one of the earliest bills seeking to restrict medically necessary care for transgender children in Texas. The legislation would have made it a crime for parents to help their children access gender-affirming care, defining it as "child abuse." Clutching her phone and reading her prepared remarks at a table before the Texas Senate Committee on State Affairs, Amber stated, "I'm afraid that by speaking here today that my words will be used against me should [these bills] pass, and my sweet son whom I love more than life itself will be taken from me." She went on to share how much Grayson was thriving: "This is possible because he has parents who affirm him and provide him the support he needs. Taking that support away from him—or worse, taking him away from his family because we broke the law to provide the support—will have devastating, heart-breaking consequences. If these bills become law, *that*, Senators, is child abuse. And I promise that I will call every one of you every single time a transgender child dies by suicide to remind you that their lives could have been saved, but you chose not to."[10]

Across Texas, other families prepared for the reality that DFPS might investigate them. Mike and Becca Robinson, the couple from chapter one who are preparing to move their son Jaxon to California, were one of them. Becca was glued to the news about the directive. The family had also read about the Briggles and their pending DFPS investigation. "We thought it was all political theater at first," Becca says. "But then we heard about the actual investigations happening, and it was scary."

Mike, who is a lawyer, wrote a letter for Jaxon to carry with him in his backpack. "We sat him down, and at ten years old, explained to him that the government here is bad and doing something evil, and they are trying to hurt children who are transgender. If anyone comes to your school and wants to talk to you about being transgender, you give them this letter, and you say you want them to talk to your parents. We have to protect you. And we will protect you."

•

Just a few years prior to being investigated due to Attorney General Ken Paxton's anti-trans memo, Amber and Adam had actually invited Paxton to join their family for dinner.

In the summer of 2016, Amber and Adam had gone to Fort Worth to listen to lawyers from Paxton's office deliver arguments in their case against the Obama Administration's Department of Education, which had issued guidance to states saying that discriminating against transgender students was a violation of the federal Title IX law prohibiting discrimination based on sex. "On a whim, we decided to go down there and be visible," Amber recalls. It was one of their first forays into activism, and Grayson was featured briefly in a news segment about the hearing. Amber had recently joined Twitter (now X), where she connected with a few of the reporters she met at the courthouse. A few weeks later, when the court ruling came out (from a far-right judge that regularly ruled against LGBTQ+ equality), the reporters asked for Amber's reaction. A reporter from NBC let Amber know that she planned on interviewing Attorney General Paxton later that day and asked if Amber and Adam had anything they wanted to say to him? "I asked if she could invite him to dinner on my behalf—because we knew that if he came to meet us and meet Grayson, he would say that trans kids are not the boogeyman he thinks they are," Amber says. "I figured this was all just a big misunderstanding—that he didn't know any transgender people—and so I wanted to introduce him."

Amber joked about the invitation and took to Twitter with humorous tweets about the hypothetical dinner. *What should she wear? Should she ask Mrs. Paxton to bring dessert?*

But a few days later, the NBC reporter said that the attorney general had accepted Amber's invitation. He and his wife came to their home (Mrs. Paxton did, in fact, bring a dessert), and they all shared a lovely two-and-a-half-hour dinner. At the end of the meal, Amber later told *The Texas Tribune*, she asked Attorney General Paxton to do everything he could to support transgender kids like her son. He merely shrugged and said that the attorney general's job is to enforce laws—not make them.

•

Amber and Adam joined one of several lawsuits against Paxton's directive, and soon after, a federal judge ruled that the directive was not enforceable against any of the plaintiff families—including anyone who identified as a member of PFLAG, which is involved in one of the lawsuits.[11] (PFLAG is a national organization—with local chapters—that provides supportive programs for LGBTQ+ people and their families and friends; the lawsuit was filed after the Office of the Attorney General of Texas requested records and documents related to PFLAG's work with transgender youth and their families.[12, 13]) But even with the directive on hold, it created a chilling effect across the state and continued to harm the families of transgender children.

One of the parents who felt the effects was Danielle, whose family in Austin was featured in chapter one. Three days after the ban took effect in September 2023, Danielle received a call from DFPS. Someone had reported her household and accused Danielle of child abuse. Danielle and her partner were asked to take a drug test, and their home was thoroughly searched. Peter, Danielle's fourteen-year-old son, and his younger brother were interviewed separately. "Can you tell me the names of drugs?" the DFPS agent asked the two of them. "Just list as many as you can."

Danielle was shocked and terrified and didn't know what the search was about. The investigator eventually showed

Danielle some paperwork that she said included accusations of drug use, as well as suspicions that Danielle was raising her child to be transgender.

Fortunately, the situation was quickly resolved; the adults passed the drug test, nothing in the house was cited, and the investigator said that she would close the case. But the afternoon was a scary one—adding trauma to an already tumultuous time for Danielle and Peter.

•

While the anti-transgender bans take a massive toll on transgender youth as well as their parents or caregivers, they also cause damage to everyone in their orbit—including the siblings of the transgender children. Amber and Adam think that's an important piece of the story that advocates for transgender dignity and equality don't often think about. And they've seen it firsthand with their youngest child, Mae. "Grayson is fine—he's like the eye of a hurricane," Amber says. "But people don't think about when a DFPS caseworker comes into your home, or when a bill is passed and you have to travel hundreds of miles for healthcare—that affects Grayson and it affects us, but it affects everyone around him, including his sibling, Mae. It bothers me that people don't think about how these anti-trans policies hurt her, too. She *also* has to sit through these terrible legislative hearings. She *also* had to endure that DFPS investigation. But no one asks about her and how she's been impacted. "Mae doesn't recall much about the investigation. "I was scared, and my parents told me not to answer questions," she says. "I remember that the woman asked me what my cats' names were—but I think I blocked the rest out of my memory."

"That's a lot to process when you're nine years old," Amber points out. "Like you're just coming out of COVID, and the world's scary, and then someone comes to say that they're gonna take your family apart? It's awful."

•

"You have to protect minorities from the tyranny of the majority," Alexia Korberg says. "When you have these new laws that are doing these wacky things that they've never done before and they're all targeting this group that is so disfavored . . . that's a pretty good red flag that something unconstitutional is happening."

District Court Judge Lynn Winmill's decision on *Poe v. Labrador* seemed to support this. In December 2023, he ruled that the law violated the Due Process Clause and Equal Protection Clause of the Fourteenth Amendment,[14] writing that "[t]ime and again, these cases illustrate that the Fourteenth Amendment's primary role is to protect disfavored minorities and preserve our fundamental rights from legislative overreach. That was true for newly freed slaves following the Civil War.

It was true in the Twentieth Century for women, people of color, interracial couples, and individuals seeking access to contraception. And it is no less true for transgender children and their parents in the Twenty-First Century."[15]

"The Idaho ban has a ten-year penalty for violating the law. That's ten years in prison," Alexia says. "That's the same as multiple types of manslaughter under the Idaho penal code." In other words, breaking the law—by following the standard of care that is supported by every major medical organization in the United States—would be "categorized as a crime of violence."

When we interviewed Alexia in February 2024, Idaho's gender-affirming care ban had yet to go into effect. The Ninth Circuit Court of Appeals supported blocking enforcement of the law while the state's appeal was decided. A few weeks before Alexia's interview, though, the state of Idaho applied for a partial stay against the injunction that was blocking the enforcement of the ban. When we spoke, there was still no word from the Supreme Court in what Alexia says should be "an easy decision." Then, in late April, the Supreme Court issued a surprise decision allowing the ban to go into effect for all trans Idahoans—except for the two plaintiffs involved in the case. (How this will be enforced is unclear, as the two plaintiffs are anonymous, and doctors who violate the law face up to ten years of imprisonment.)

We asked Alexia if they thought that the Idaho case—or

another case on gender-affirming care bans—would ultimately go to the Supreme Court for a final decision. With so many different laws and lawsuits coming up across the United States, they said yes. (In June 2024, several months after we spoke to Alexia, the Supreme Court granted review in a case challenging Tennessee's ban.)

We wondered if Alexia was hopeful about the outcome.

"I think that there are so many people on the Supreme Court who . . . have a reverence for the law," they say. "And all I can do is hope that, ultimately, their reverence for the law . . . is heavier on the scale of their deliberation than their personal politics."

What gives them even more hope, though, are trans kids themselves.

When Alexia was two years old, their earliest words were "I'm not a girl." Still, it took them decades to come out about their trans identity, which they describe as "the most enduring facet" of who they are.

Today, they admire trans youth, who are being themselves, exploring their identities, and teaching the world about gender liberation and expansiveness—explorations that they say help cisgender people as well as those who are trans.

"The kids are great," Alexia says. "And as an adult, I'm just trying to do the best I can to make it safer for them to be them."

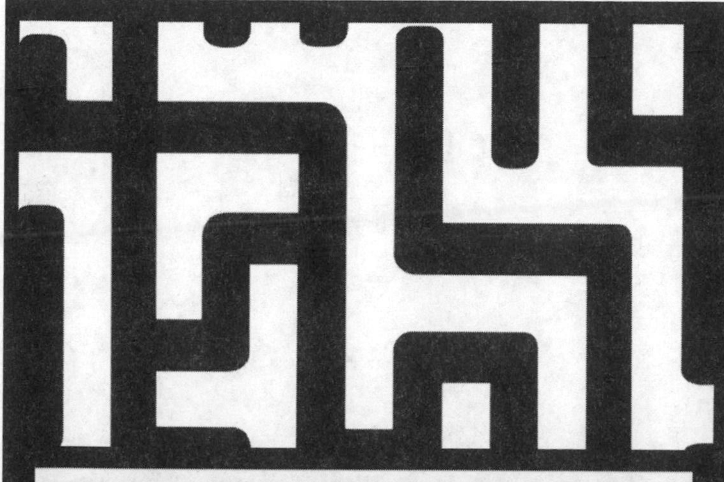

PART II: FINDING YOUR WAY

Chapter Five

"I just wanted a healthy, happy, whole baby," says Amber Briggle, remembering her pregnancy with her first child, Grayson. "That's all I wanted."

Adam Briggle recalled something his father used to say whenever he'd meet a new baby. "You know how people say, like, 'Oh, she looks like you,' or 'she looks like her aunt,' or whatever?" Adam says. "My dad would always say, 'He looks just like himself.' It's like, this is a human being with an open life journey in front of him, and whatever expectations you've got are only that. So I never really pegged a lot on figuring out who Grayson was going to be. I just wanted to enjoy the ride with them."

Adam and Amber didn't have to wait too long for Grayson to tell them who he was. "He came out as soon as he could talk," Amber recalls. She was driving him home from school, and the teacher had let her know that Grayson was especially well-behaved that day. "Miss Lucy said you were such a good girl today at school, and I'm so proud of you," Amber told Grayson.

"I'm not a girl!" Grayson responded. "I am a boy, and I like Spider-Man."

"You know, girls can also like Spider-Man—and there are a lot of different ways that girls can be," Amber answered, wanting to nip any gender stereotyping in the bud. "You don't have to love glittery painted nails and all things pink to be a girl."

It didn't matter: "I am a boy. And I like Spider-Man," Grayson asserted.

"I was just trying to redefine what it meant to be a girl," Amber recalls sixteen years later. "You know, super fucking woke feminist, right?"

Grayson had always gravitated more toward action figures and athletics and more traditionally "boy" toys. As a toddler, he often opted out of participating in the rec center ballet class that Amber signed him up for because a bucket of trucks seemed more interesting. "We were still able to get him in dresses at that point—but with lots of struggle," Amber shares. "And I remember looking at the class, and there were these cute little girls in pink tutus doing their thing, and Grayson was sitting in the corner playing with his fire truck. He would only do ballet if Adam joined the circle of girls—because then, he was doing something with his dad."

When Grayson was four, he asked his mom a question from the backseat of the car while she was pulling into the driveway:

"Do you think scientists could turn me into a boy?"

"There was a sadness or a longing in his voice," Amber remembers. "It wasn't like, 'Hey, do you think we could go to the moon someday?' It was more of a sincere yearning than a curious question."

"What do you mean?" Amber asked. "Is that something you want?"

Grayson nodded. And Amber only had one thought: "Well, I've got some research to do."

One of Adam and Amber's friends from church at the time was an out transgender man, and they asked him for guidance on how to best support their young gender nonconforming child. Between his advice and the information from the limited research that was available, including academic journals and a handful of resources from LGBTQ+ support groups, Adam and Amber learned that they should simply allow Grayson to express himself the way he wanted to and resist putting any pressure on him when it came to identity or expression.

Grayson continued to prefer boys' clothes and masculine haircuts, and it got to the point where strangers began referring to him as a boy. "At five and six years old, he would hold the door for people, and they'd stop and say, 'Oh, what a nice gentleman you are,' or 'What a handsome young man.' I, however, continued to interrupt them to explain that Grayson was a girl and that there were lots of ways to be a polite and great girl. Everyone would feel super shut down in those moments. They were just strangers who were trying to say something nice."

The person who felt most shut down in those moments, though, was Grayson. "Looking back, I can see that he felt betrayed by his mother—after all, I was the one misgendering him, not the strangers."

•

When LJ's youngest child, Aaren, was a toddler, LJ (a member of a Native nation) wondered if Aaren might grow up to be gender expansive. Though Aaren was assigned female at birth, from a very young age, he told his parents he was a "he."

"My boy has always been a boy," says LJ, who uses they/she pronouns. LJ tells the story of when Aaren first told them exactly who he was: When Aaren was three, he and his dad were standing outside, watching Aaren's older siblings get on a school bus. "One day, you'll be on a bus," Aaren's dad said. "What do you think about that?"

"I don't know if I would like it," Aaren answered.

Aaren's dad was surprised. "Why not?" he asked. "Is the bus too big? Do you think it'll go too fast?"

Aaren shook his head. "I don't think the boys will like me."

"Why do you think the boys won't like you?"

"Because I don't think they'll think I'm a real boy."

Aaren's dad took a deep breath. "I can see how that would

make you not want to ride the bus," he said. "But I don't think that'll happen, you know. I think you'll have a bus driver that'll make sure you'll be okay."

When LJ and their spouse talked about this later, one of LJ's first thoughts was, "How is he so small and he's got these big feelings of not being accepted?" Aaren had also been calling himself "he" instead of "she" for months.

LJ, who is Two-Spirit and Indigiqueer, said that her tribe believes children come from the stars—and "they choose us."

"So now we've got to take our cue from them," she says.

So LJ and her spouse did. They started using "he/him" pronouns with Aaren. They told their families about what was going on. When one of Aaren's grandfathers met the news with a gentle, "Oh, okay," LJ felt like, "We can do this."

•

When Grayson was in first grade, Adam and Amber received a call from Grayson's teacher requesting a meeting. The teacher had flagged that Grayson was having some behavioral issues—he was extremely fidgety during story time, wasn't paying attention during lessons, and hid behind the door or under a table when it came time for the class to line up and get ready for dismissal or bathroom time. "Grayson was just such a rule follower, and we'd never had issues before, so it was a bit concerning," Amber recalls. "And the teacher even said that for a lot of first graders, it was fairly normal behavior, but it was out of character for Grayson."

A few weeks passed, but the behavior persisted, and Amber started noticing that after school, when he was dropped off at her small business, Grayson would immediately run to the bathroom. What's more, he went right past the women's bathroom, which was closer, and into the men's room.

Then one day, right before Grayson's seventh birthday, "it just kind of all clicked for me," Amber says. "One night I was tucking Grayson into bed, and we were having a sweet moment—he was all shiny because he just had his bath, and he was wearing cute little jammies, and I asked him, 'Is there something you want to tell me? Should I be calling you my son and not my daughter? Is there a different name you want to go by?'"

Grayson's face lit up. And he immediately said that he wanted to go by his initials. Amber then asked about the bathroom situation.

"If I go into the girls' bathroom, people who don't know me think I'm in the wrong bathroom because of how I look," Grayson shared. "And if I go to the boys' bathroom, people who *do* know me think I'm in the wrong bathroom. I don't really know where to go, so I just hold it."

That made a lot of sense to Amber—and it explained some of the behavioral issues: of course he couldn't sit still—plus his grades were slipping—because he had to think about his bladder all day.

"I love you so much," Amber told him. "Now, go to bed. I'm going to make all of this right."

Amber and Adam met with the school principal, who said that Grayson could use the bathroom in the nurse's office since that was where he felt most comfortable at the time. Within three weeks, Grayson's reading comprehension and grades had jumped multiple levels. He could finally concentrate now that he wasn't so concerned about where or when he'd be able to relieve himself.

By second grade, Grayson had been socially presenting as a boy for a while and started preferring to use the boys' room. The nurse's bathroom was a further walk from his class, and he started feeling singled out by and different by having to walk there every time he needed to use the bathroom. "Baby, just go to the bathroom," Amber told Grayson one day, and he started using the boys' room.

The school called and flagged that he needed to use the nurse's bathroom.

"Thank you for that option," Amber told the school.

"It's not an option," they replied.

"I know everyone at the ACLU," Amber said. And the school backed down.

•

By the time Aaren entered pre-kindergarten at a local public school, he was a boy like any other boy.

But Aaren and his family live in rural Oklahoma—in a two-stoplight town with a grocery store, a Dollar General, and not much else. It was only a matter of time before the state's anti-transgender policies began impacting the family.

In Aaren's first year of school, in 2021, everything seemed like it might be okay. The principal was supportive and discreet, and Aaren's teacher had taught a gender-diverse child at a previous school.

But in 2022, a bathroom ban passed in Oklahoma that required students to use restrooms that aligned with the sex on their birth certificates.[1] Students who declined to use such bathrooms had to use "a single-occupancy restroom or changing room" provided by the school. If a school district failed to comply, they risked a percentage of their state funding getting cut—and they could also be sued by parents.[2]

That fall, Aaren started kindergarten. The nearest single-occupancy bathroom was on the other side of the school. LJ was concerned. "What if he's worried about peeing on himself and he wants to go to the closest bathroom?" she asked at the time. "What if he gets caught?" While the principal said that the school wasn't going to punish Aaren, LJ believed it was "just stupid that we had to think through this." Fortunately, by the start of the next school year in 2023, the school had moved Aaren's classroom closer to the single-occupancy restroom.

Despite this, Aaren still doesn't always understand why he can't just use the boys' bathroom.

As new discriminatory laws come down the pipeline, LJ worries how they'll stay on top of them—and protect Aaren's privacy, autonomy, and identity. "There's so much, and you're just trying to do right by your children," they say.

•

Satya Azadi and her twelve-year-old child, Rishta, live in a mid-sized city in Virginia. Satya first enrolled Rishta in a small private school because Satya is lesbian, and she wanted her child to attend a school where LGBTQ+ families would be affirmed and supported. Later, when Rishta was nine years old, she came out as genderfluid. Now, at twelve, she identifies as trans and lesbian (using she/they pronouns).

Rishta has attended both public and private schools—and all have had their challenges.

"It's hard because it's also intersectional," Satya says. At the schools they've attended, "someone can get the stuff about gender or sexuality but not get it about race." For example, at a public elementary school that Rishta went to, the teacher asked the students to write a public service announcement about anything they wanted. Rishta wrote about LGBTQ+ issues. The teacher "reprimanded her and was like, 'That's not what I asked you to do,'" Satya recalls.

Soon after, Rishta went back to private school, where she came out as genderfluid. She had to educate both teachers and students about what "genderfluid" was, and kids sometimes made fun of her. When the board of directors of the school hired a principal with a very conservative Christian background, Satya rallied other LGBTQ+ families to share their concerns—only to be silenced by the school's leadership.

When Rishta moved to her current school in 2023, at the start of sixth grade, both she and their mother were hopeful. The teachers wore pronoun pins, and there were other LGBTQ+ families—as well as out queer staff. When Rishta asked to change their name during the fall semester, the school counselor and administration helped them do so.

Yet, there are few Black and Brown families at the new school. And every day, Satya worries about the physical and political violence that threaten her and her child—both as a queer and trans family and as Indian Americans, one of whom is an immigrant. She hears Rishta's stories—the transphobic things their classmates say, or the group text where the brunt of the (primarily White) kids' jokes devolved into emojis with bindis, nose rings, and Brown skin ("very much directed at Rishta in a very exaggerated and caricatured way," Satya says). When Rishta tried to talk to their peers about why that wasn't okay, they were kicked out of the group chat.

"It's really hard . . . seeing your child experience this on a daily basis," Satya shares. "Everybody else just gets to be a regular student in school, but my kid doesn't."

For the last two years, Satya tried to leave Virginia, applying for jobs in different states. But in early 2024, she decided to stick it out. She'll make her own bubble of queer, trans, and affirming community and try to make it work.

In the meantime, Rishta will continue going to the private school they've chosen. Satya knows it could be far worse—at least the school's administration is supportive.

•

The stories shared in this chapter reveal a common theme for many of the families of transgender youth: in their day-to-day lives, they experience tremendous support and affirmation from their families, friends, teachers, and other individuals who are around them and actually know them. However, outside of this cocoon of support lies a world of hostility—due to things such as statewide anti-trans legislation, national anti-trans rhetoric, and liminal online spaces.

"We've been incredibly fortunate," Adam Briggle says. "We've had so much support from the people that really matter in our lives. That's why it's so infuriating to have that other side of the coin with the legislatures and the online bullies—because it's just so obvious that they're coming from a place of ignorance. The limits of rational persuasion hit pretty quickly when people are not part of the lived experience of raising a trans child."

When Grayson came out as transgender, his family told

everyone who needed to know: his teachers, their family, fellow congregants in their church (mostly so they would not accidentally misgender Grayson). "It was not a big deal," Amber shares. "He just continued to be himself, only a million percent happier."

When the Texas legislature started pushing anti-transgender bills, statewide advocacy groups including Equality Texas and the Transgender Education Network of Texas reached out to the Briggles. Many Texans had heard the family's story about inviting Attorney General Paxton over to dinner, which news outlets across the state covered widely at the time.[3] "It just took off from there," Amber says. Her website, where she published charming essays about parenting, running a small business, and more, became popular and widely read. Her Twitter account, which was sometimes funny, sometimes outraged, and sometimes both at the same time, amassed thousands of followers. As a result, the family was frequently called on to comment on transgender issues in Texas and, eventually, on the national level. Amber and Adam participated in panel discussions, and they shared their family's story in news articles and on TV. "It's not that our story is that remarkable—it's just that we were one of the first," Amber says, explaining that at the time, there were very few families in Texas speaking publicly about parenting trans youth.

It wasn't until anti-LGBTQ+ lawmakers began targeting transgender youth for exclusion and discrimination that many families of transgender youth felt the urgent need to speak up and push back.

In 2017, lawmakers in Texas introduced legislation blocking transgender people from using restrooms aligned with their gender identity. The bill was similar to several previous bills introduced in Texas. A 2015 bill aimed to criminalize transgender students for using the restroom that aligned with their gender identity and would have required schools to pay $2,000 plus damages to cisgender students who accused their trans peers of breaking the law.[4] Another 2015 bill would have convicted trans people over the age of thirteen of a misdemeanor if they used the "wrong" restroom, with a penalty of up to one year in jail and a $4,000 fine.[5] Neither bill passed.

The Briggles spoke out publicly about the 2017 legislation, with Amber appearing on panel discussions about transgender equality[6] and the family attending a Trans Texas Lobby Day where they met with legislators. At one point during the Lobby Day, Grayson broke down in tears. The *San Antonio Express-News* ran a photo of Amber comforting Grayson, which Amber posted on social media, writing: "Can I just admit for a second how effing tired I am of having to comfort my baby and protect him from bullies in Austin? Let me just be real for a second. This sucks so hard. He deserves a summer vacation with his friends, not a political pissing contest with the Texas Legislature. Not fair. I'm mad as hell."[7] The photo went viral and was seen by millions.

In anticipation of the "bathroom bill," which looked like it would be railroaded to passage, Amber and Adam proceeded with a name and gender marker change for Grayson, ensuring that legal documents like his birth certificate and Social Security card reflected his accurate name and gender. "As long as we're going to pass laws saying which facilities you can and can't use, it's awfully nice to have a document saying he can use it," Amber told reporters. "At the same time, I just feel like it's so unnecessary. Why do I have to change my son's birth certificate so he can be treated like the boy that he is?"[8]

The Briggles have shown up in Austin again and again and again over the past several years, testifying against a battery of dangerous legislation—from the bathroom bill in 2017 (which ultimately did not pass) to the "child abuse" bill in 2021 to the ban on medically necessary health care for trans youth in 2023. "I have been counting down the legislative sessions in Texas," Adam says (the legislature meets every other year). "There's really only one more session until Grayson graduates. I'm hopeful that we will personally be able to get through the gauntlet here."

In their advocacy, the Briggles have heard one question more than any other: "Why stay in Texas?" For the family, it's not a simple calculus: Adam is a tenured university professor in a workforce where those positions are not widely available, while Amber has a small business with dozens of employees. If they switch or quit jobs, what happens to their health insurance? Their retirement fund? Their college fund for the kids? "We don't really have a choice right now," Amber says. "We're kind of, for the lack of a better word, stuck here. I would like to be in a place, financially, where we can choose to be here if that's what we choose."

Beyond that, they have also resisted moving because this is where their lives are. "We're here because this is where Grayson likes to be—not Texas, but our community here," Adam explains. Adam and Amber both referenced that they've heard of families who have moved to "blue" states that have reputations for being more welcoming, and while there may not specifically be anti-transgender laws in those places, the families have often reported that it's been hard to identify a supportive, affirming school district or to build community. "Grayson is doing so well in school, he's got a bazillion friends, he's got, like, a 4.2 GPA," Amber says. "The kid has two and a half years left of high school. Why would we pull him from this otherwise very accepting and supportive environment that he's experiencing on a daily basis?"

"It's almost like we are in this protective bubble, like a capsule, inside of an acidic stomach," Adam adds. "And we're just hoping this capsule holds long enough."

•

Since the early 2020s, hundreds of bills have been proposed in state legislatures across the US that impact LGBTQ+ people in schools—including students, faculty, and staff. These have included "Don't Say LGBTQ+" bills that censor discussions of trans and queer topics; policies that prohibit trans students from playing on sports teams that align with their gender identity; bills that require staff and administrators to out their students to parents; bills allowing staff to "deadname" and use the wrong pronouns for students; bills that explicitly prohibit students from using bathrooms that align with their gender identities; and bills that ban or restrict access to books or materials about LGBTQ+ people or topics.[9,10] At the beginning of the 2023 school year, thirty new laws went into effect in fifteen states.[11] As of early 2024, 192 bills impacting LGBTQ+ students' and teachers' rights had been proposed in forty states.[12]

Oklahoma has been one of the worst states in terms of anti-transgender legislation. In 2021, the state passed a law that banned teaching about systemic inequality in public K–12 schools (including accurately teaching about the Tulsa Race Massacre and the Trail of Tears).[13] The State Board of Education also passed a rule forcing K–12 schools to submit their library catalogs for review—and the rule has been used to ban or censor books with LGBTQ+ themes.[14] As of 2022, trans girls were banned from participating in girls' sports at public schools.[15] In 2023, the State Board of Education mandated that school staff notify parents if a student requests any change to their gender identity, and in January 2024, they unanimously passed a rule that effectively prohibits school districts from altering a student's recorded gender.[16]

The Oklahoma Superintendent of Public Instruction, Ryan Walters, has made his anti-transgender stance clear. "We're not going to do the transgender game of back and forth, back and forth," he said during a Board of Education meeting in October 2023. "We have two genders. Those are the genders that are set."[17]

The deluge of anti-trans policies in Oklahoma continues to grow—to the point where, for parents like LJ, they're hard to keep track of. In January 2024, a bill was introduced in the state House of Representatives (HB 3120) that would prohibit school faculty and staff from using a student's preferred pronouns if they don't correspond to their assigned sex at birth.[18] The law would also penalize public school employees for asking students what pronouns they use. As of April 2024, HB 3120 was one of seven anti-LGBTQ+ bills advancing in Oklahoma's state legislature.[19]

And the hostility goes beyond actual legislation. In multiple conversations with parents of trans and gender nonconforming youth, Nex Benedict's name came up. Nex (Choctaw) was a young trans person of Indigenous descent who died in Oklahoma after being bullied in a school bathroom (sources close to Nex have said that he used he/they pronouns and identified as transgender).[20,21,22] Though the Oklahoma Medical

Examiner ruled the death suicide, as of spring 2024, many questions remained—and regardless of what happened, Nex's death sent aftershocks of grief and anger throughout LGBTQ+ communities and families.

Many parents we interviewed teared up as they spoke about Nex. For LJ, who lives in Oklahoma, his death hit particularly close to home. "It's like a grief process that you can't really prepare yourself for when you are so close to something like that," LJ says. "And it's hard to straddle a line of advocating for your kid and also trying to preserve that autonomy for him. . . . And at the same time, it's my nature to advocate for him. I mean, that's my protective spirit."

LJ is deeply frustrated by what is happening in Oklahoma, but they recognize that these unjust laws are rooted in the state and nation's foundations of colonialism and white supremacy. "We still live in a state that honors land runs," LJ says, referring to the "land runs" of the late 1800s and early 1900s in Oklahoma (and other states), when the US government dispossessed Indigenous peoples of their lands and distributed them to mostly White settlers.[23,24,25]

While the state was built on white settler colonialism, LJ understands the power of collective movement building—and of the Indigenous communities around them—and wonders what kind of pressure Native peoples might apply to Oklahoma schools and the state government. LJ cites two resolutions passed in 2015 and 2016, respectively, by the

National Congress of American Indians (NCAI) that protect Two-Spirit people in Tribal communities. NCAI is one of the oldest and largest American Indian and Alaska Native organizations, representing 145 Tribal Nations as of 2023.[26] In the 2015 resolution, NCAI declared its "support of the full equality of all tribal persons, including two spirit, lesbian, gay, bisexual, and transgender tribal citizens, in the interest of furthering the cause of human rights and the principle of nondiscrimination for all our citizens wherever they reside" and committed to promoting nondiscrimination and supporting member tribes in pursuing governmental policies for LGBTQ+ justice. Toward the end of the resolution, they emphasized the connections between colonization and LGBTQ+ oppression: "because tribal nations, two spirit equality, and decolonization are inextricably linked, one cannot be truly achieved without the other."[27]

Building on this, in 2016, the NCAI created a Two Spirit Task Force "to assist in the coordination, collaboration, and outreach to Indian Country on Two Spirit issues; and to develop and share approaches and solutions to policy issues that affect Two Spirit/LGBT community members in a manner consistent with the Indian self-determination."[28]

NCAI "was unanimously like, 'Yes—Two-Spirit relatives, we got you,'" LJ says. "Now you're in Oklahoma with thirty-nine Tribal jurisdictions. And what are they doing? Maybe they are in negotiations. Maybe they're having conversations. . . .

[But] you all committed to this. I've been wondering—how do you leverage cultural sovereignty in a meaningful way so that the state doesn't just run us down?"

At the same time, LJ wishes that parents and caregivers of gender-expansive youth could have more support. "Not because we don't know how [to support our kids]," LJ says. "But because we're being attacked."

•

As we have seen with many of the stories in this book, the passage of anti-transgender laws has significantly shaped where some families with transgender kids wish to live.

For Margaret Tremblay, anti-trans legislation was a major factor in decision-making for her family. Her husband served in the United States Air Force, and a few years ago, while based in Massachusetts, they looked into a military program that allows families to restrict where they can be asked to move based on their access to medical care. Margaret and her husband have three children, including a sixteen-year-old son, Rowan, who is transgender, and a six-year-old son, Ollie, who has epilepsy. "We were definitely tracking the anti-LGBTQ+ policies," Margaret says. "And I was trying to match epilepsy care with gender management care."

The family created a list of "do not travel" states three

different times, although they never wound up needing to specify their preferences for military purposes since, in 2022, Margaret's husband decided to retire.

The family then decided to return home to North Carolina—Rowan was born in Cary, Ollie was born in Chapel Hill, and the family had previously been stationed at Fort Liberty in Fayetteville. They knew that North Carolina had passed HB 2, the so-called "bathroom bill," back in 2016—but there had been such a fierce backlash to it that key parts of the law had already been repealed or expired. In addition, the state had changed a lot since then. The governor was now a Democrat, and there wasn't any threat of anti-LGBTQ+ legislation passing in 2022. "I've known for the majority of my sentience that there are and have been anti-trans bills," Rowan shares. "I started to see what looked like the beginnings of this giant uptick in anti-trans legislation all across the country—and then came the summer of 2023, and it all happened in rapid succession."

Included in that rapid succession of setbacks was a major political reversal in North Carolina: a legislator who was elected to the General Assembly as a Democrat changed her party affiliation, giving Republicans enough votes to have a supermajority. Overnight, the possibility of a balanced political climate was upended. By August 2023, the North Carolina General Assembly had passed an anti-transgender school sports bill, a ban on the initiation of gender-affirming care for transgender youth, and a "Don't Say LGBTQ+"-style curriculum censorship bill.[29] "Seeing those laws pass was so upsetting," Margaret says. "And it's particularly upsetting and mind-boggling because we just moved here, and it felt like my kids' rights were immediately being eroded away by people calling themselves patriots. If we were still on active duty, the military wouldn't even station us here due to these laws."

Thankfully, Rowan was already receiving gender-affirming care in North Carolina, so he could continue seeing his doctor due to language in the healthcare ban that exempted individuals who had initiated treatment prior to the bill's enactment. "I was less worried for myself after learning about that exemption," Rowan says. "But I was worried for friends or people in the state who hadn't yet started care or were in the process of getting it set up. We actually gave up an appointment with our provider so that a new patient could have it and qualify for the exemption."

Margaret and Rowan were especially concerned about the "Don't Say LGBTQ+" law. Ollie is an elementary school student in the specific age range that is impacted by the censorship portions of the bill (which are supposed to impact kindergarten through fourth grades). Under the law, would he be blocked from sharing information or stories about his family, including his brother Rowan?

One of the problems with these school censorship laws is that they are often vaguely worded. For example, Florida's law specifically states that "classroom instruction by school personnel or third parties on sexual orientation or gender identity may not occur in kindergarten through grade three or in a manner that is not age appropriate or developmentally appropriate for students in accordance with state standards." However, Florida lawmakers did not define the terms "age appropriate," "developmentally appropriate," and "classroom instruction."[30] (In early 2024, the state reached a settlement with civil rights attorneys clarifying the language, and as of April 2024, students and teachers can discuss sexual orientation and gender identity as long as it's not part of formal instruction.)[31]

Like the SB 8 anti-abortion law in Texas, "Don't Say LGBTQ+" laws often deputize everyday citizens to enforce them—and allow parents to bring private lawsuits against school districts that violate the law.[32] Vague wording coupled with a fear of lawsuits often cows faculty and staff into overcompliance. For example, teachers might remove LGBTQ+ content that *could be* developmentally appropriate, in case someone deems it otherwise. Or a trans teacher might feel pressure to closet themself, or students, like Ollie, might be afraid to talk about their trans family members.

Notably, one of the provisions of the "Don't Say LGBTQ+" law in North Carolina requires school personnel to notify parents about changes in the name or pronoun used for a student at school.[33] It effectively forces schools to "out" transgender kids—potentially before they may be ready.

Rowan knows what that feels like. In sixth grade, at a parent-teacher conference, his social studies teacher told Margaret and her husband that Rowan was using a different name and pronouns at school. Rowan had already told Margaret that he was exploring his gender identity but hadn't told his dad. Luckily, he accepted it in stride, and they later had a conversation with Rowan to let him know they loved and supported him. "It's stressful—because that is something you choose to tell other people," Rowan says. "It's up to each individual to share or not share, so it's frustrating when that gets taken away. And even though I knew that my parents are supportive, it wasn't something I was ready to talk about . . . and then I *had* to be ready because the decision was taken away from me. I was lucky to have parents who are supportive, but there could also be a very good reason why people are not coming out to their parents—maybe they wouldn't be safe at home."

Margaret has seen firsthand the dangerous impacts of hostile homes. She used to serve as a CASA (Court Appointed Special Advocate) for children in at-risk homes. When kids are ready to come out—when they believe it will be a safe, affirming, and positive experience, she believes, they should come out. But the choice should be theirs, not their school administration's.

Beyond this, Margaret thinks that "forced outing" policies won't actually provide parents with more information about their kids. "They're in effect making it less likely that the kids are going to tell their parents—because when the kids are talking to somebody like a trusted adult who they feel safe with, chances are that person is supporting them and also encouraging them to reach out to people in their lives who may support them as well. If that child is not comfortable with coming out to their parents, and they have no other safe adult to talk to or to help them work through this, that can be a dangerous situation. It's really removing a safeguard for some kids."

In the leadup to the slate of legislation that passed in North Carolina in 2023—and in its aftermath—Margaret and Rowan spoke out as best as they could. They testified before legislators against the healthcare ban. Margaret spoke at a press conference outside of the North Carolina General Assembly on the day of a key floor vote. They shared their story with reporters because they wanted more people in North Carolina and nationwide to understand the danger of these political attacks. "That's what really empowered me to speak out," Rowan says. "I have a lot of privilege as a trans person because I have acceptance, and I still have my healthcare. I thought that I should use that privilege to speak out and help those who don't have it."

•

One of the most important tools for advocating against anti-LGBTQ+ laws is the media. The more that people can see transgender people for who they really are—happy, thriving, and not the false caricatures frequently painted by conservatives—the greater the chances of acceptance, and ultimately, success for the LGBTQ+ movement in this country.

An excellent example of media-savvy trans advocates are Harleigh and her father, Jeff. They are from Auburn, Alabama, and for the most part, live relatively ordinary lives—they like to have cookouts, Jeff likes to take the family out on the lake in his little boat, and every December they decorate their house with Christmas lights so extravagant that the whole town comes to see them. "When you look [us up] on the internet now, you find two things: advocacy stuff, and all the Christmas lights," Jeff laughs. "But getting involved in advocacy was accidental."

In 2020, at the height of the COVID-19 pandemic, the family began joining virtual meetings through their local PFLAG chapter. It was a positive environment with lots of resources and people sharing stories about their journey—including Harleigh's exposure to extreme bullying that resulted in her family pulling her from school in sixth grade and enrolling her in virtual classes for a year.

During one meeting in 2021, the regional director of PFLAG asked if any families in Alabama would be interested in sharing their story with the media in response to the proposed ban on gender-affirming care in the state. Harleigh and Jeff agreed to do it. "We said, maybe we should try it, and let's see what it's like," Jeff recalls. "It was like a father-daughter bonding thing." They ended up being interviewed by the BBC,[34] which left Harleigh and Jeff feeling empowered. "We found that we were capable of doing it," Jeff says, "and we know that not everyone can do media or feels safe enough to do it, so we decided that we would be okay with putting ourselves out there."

"I am privileged to have such a supportive family, being trans," Harleigh adds. "So I wanted to take the opportunity to advocate for trans kids—because we need those voices right now."

Jeff now serves as the vice president of his local PFLAG chapter, and he—and Harleigh—are proud to help families of transgender youth living in Alabama and other states. For example, when the healthcare ban was proposed in Alabama in 2021, Harleigh and Jeff spoke out repeatedly, sharing virtual testimony against the ban, and lobbying as much as possible in person. They spent Harleigh's spring break in Montgomery, speaking with legislators, including the governor's chief health advisor. Harleigh had been receiving medical care for several years by then, and if the ban passed and took effect, the family would be put in an especially challenging spot, as Harleigh's brother—"one of Harleigh's biggest cheerleaders," Jeff says—was midway through a six-year term with the Alabama National Guard. The healthcare ban was forcing the family to choose between two terrible options: stay in Alabama to be close to their son, at the expense of Harleigh's healthcare, or move elsewhere to continue Harleigh's care but split up the family in the process. (When the law passed, they joined a lawsuit against it as plaintiffs.)[35]

Their advocacy journey has continued beyond Alabama. In 2023, Harleigh became the youngest person to testify before the United States Senate Judiciary Committee when she shared her story as part of calling for the passage of the Equality Act, which would ensure inclusive nondiscrimination protections at the federal level.[36] "It was awe-inspiring to watch her do that," Jeff recalls with pride.

During the hearing, Harleigh, wearing a gray Madras blazer and a gold heart locket around her neck, spoke about coming out as a young trans person and experiencing bullying by her peers—as well as her state government. "I love my life. I love my family. I love my friends. And I am happy," she said. "I am asking for you to help us stop certain people from using the transgender community as a political pawn. Please stop attacking our lives for votes or money. These are human rights hanging in the balance. Help us communicate that they are impacting people's lives and our pursuit of happiness. We are just like your kids, just like your neighbors, and you. We also deserve the ability to be happy."[37]

One of the family's most prominent opportunities to advocate was on *The Kelly Clarkson Show* in 2023. On the program, they sat on a couch with actress and LGBTQ+ advocate Laverne Cox and talked about their lives in order to help viewers understand the unique challenges facing transgender youth nationwide. Jeff emphasized something that he brings up as much as he can: that despite the laws and anti-transgender hostility, transgender people who are treated with love and care can excel. "I think a lot of what gets painted in the stories in the media is that trans people are miserable in their lives," he says. "That is so far from the truth. I look at my kid, and she's happy and thriving and doing all of these incredible things—and I work with a lot of kids that don't have as much support, but they also have these pockets where they're just teenagers, and they're just kids, and they're happy."

While Harleigh and Jeff enjoy doing media appearances and special events, they both wish they weren't always in response to a negative anti-transgender advance. "It's cool to receive these invitations," Harleigh says. "But it's frustrating because the reason for those invitations is sad. I shouldn't have to be here, but I am."

The public visibility has also led to some tensions in the family's day-to-day life. In Alabama, there is a law in effect prohibiting transgender students from using the restroom that aligns with their gender identity. Even though the sponsor of the bill said that he didn't expect anyone to actually enforce the law, a parent wound up calling Harleigh's school to complain about her using the girls' restroom. The school told Harleigh that she couldn't use the girls' restroom anymore, and since she does not feel safe in the boys' bathroom, she now largely avoids using the restroom while at school.

Overall, Harleigh and Jeff describe the school's response to their public advocacy as "hot and cold"—sometimes supportive of her opportunities and accomplishments, other times, not at all. For example, right after the school met with Harleigh to inform her that she could no longer use the girls' restroom, she had to go to a debate tournament. "There was a lot going through my head, but I still did well and won the tournament in my event," she says. "And then the next Monday, I saw the school post a picture of me saying 'Harleigh Wins Debate Tournament.' It's like, okay, great, it's nice for you to celebrate me as a person and for my accomplishments. But it also kind of feels like you're treating me as less than a person, only supporting me when it helps rather than as a matter of principle. It's like they're not willing to stand by us all the way."

Harleigh was also invited to travel to Washington, DC, to meet the Vice President of the United States and Second Gentleman and share her thoughts about how the White House could better support transgender youth. "I thought this should be an excused absence—it is an incredible educational opportunity, and I think it is a testament to Auburn City Schools," Jeff says. But the school refused to excuse Harleigh's absence.

Harleigh has a little over a year left in high school—and then, Jeff expects she will likely leave the state. That's sad for the family. Jeff's office is decked out in gear from Auburn University—Auburn pennants, crests, and rally towels, along with blue and orange pom-poms. "We live five miles from one of the best colleges in the state," Jeff says. "But she cannot go to school in this state. And honestly, she has no reason to ever come back, which is what they want—they don't want the LGBTQ+ community in the state."

"Do I want to move? No," Harleigh says. "This is where I grew up. I've lived here all my life. Having to leave all of that behind because of some fearmongering politics—it's so unnecessary."

Harleigh does not know where the next few years will take her, but she does know one thing for sure: "Even if I move out of Alabama, I'm not going to stop advocating for people in Alabama—or anywhere in the country."

•

For many families, advocating against anti-transgender laws and policies can be both a blessing and a curse. While the importance of their advocacy efforts cannot be overstated, the pressures and constant public attention that come with it can create a very stressful situation—for parents *and* children.

The Briggles, for example, suspect that their high profile was one of the reasons they were investigated by the Texas DFPS in 2022. "One of the things I'm thinking a lot about is that you can be out, but you can also be out by degrees—out within certain circles and not others," Adam Briggle says. "I don't think we were sufficiently attuned to those options. We always told ourselves, maybe it's true that people need to see an example to be able to open their minds and change their opinions—and that it has to be a real name, a real face, a real family."

"There was no one out there modeling best practices for us," Amber Briggle adds. "I don't think we understood the longevity of the internet. As a family, we did talk about 'Should we do this story? Do you want to come to this event? Can we use your name?' And those first couple of months, it was cameras on me only, no permission to share pictures of the kids or their names. It was only as we got more comfortable and realized it wasn't so big and scary out there to do this work that we got a little more daring."

Adam also makes the point that, "We've heard so many times people say that kids are too young to know their gender identity. And that has not at *all* been the case. But they might be too young to understand the ramifications of media interactions."

Grayson recently expressed that he is getting frustrated with the amount of publicity. "I said, 'Grayson, we did this because I wanted to make your life better,'" Amber recalls. "And he goes, 'We've made other kids' lives better . . . But my life? Mom, you can *Google* me.'"

"I've got a lot of regrets about that," Amber says, her voice breaking. "You Google his name, and it's out there forever. And he's going to go off to college, and his roommates are going to Google his name, and now he doesn't have the opportunity to control his story. It's out there—and I will forever, *forever* regret that, until the day I die."

She and Adam offer one major piece of advice to parents

who ask for guidance on sharing their story publicly: Use a pseudonym. "You don't need to use your kids' names," Amber says. "We could have been the Bakers or the Johnsons and been just as effective doing this work."

Despite his reluctance about future public appearances, Grayson has undoubtedly found community through his advocacy. He is currently involved with The GenderCool Project, an organization dedicated to centering the stories of trans and queer youth.[38] "He loves the GenderCool Champions. They've become his friends," Adam says. "Amber asked if he wanted to go to the GLAAD Media Awards, and his first question was, 'Will there be other GenderCool Champions there?' And I said there will be, and he's like, sheepishly, 'Okay, I'll go.'"

"I think as he gets older, he's also realizing the importance of this moment in our culture," Adam says. "I think it's dawning on him, like it has on us, the real threat of a regression into a Christian nationalist country. I sometimes see stirrings in him, in his own way, of wanting to push back against that. I think he's just trying to find his voice."

•

Rishta Azadi can easily rattle off LGBTQ+ youth suicide rates (The Trevor Project reports that 41 percent of LGBTQ+ young people seriously considered attempting suicide in the past year[39]) and knows that that number drops by 40 percent when youth have at least one supportive adult in their lives.[40] She also closely tracks the destruction in Palestine and voices outrage about the more than 30,000 Palestinians—and counting—who are dead in Gaza. "The sliver of hope that I have is small acts of rebellion," Rishta says. "But right now I don't feel that much hope."

But their mother, Satya, disagrees. Recently, she saw a video of a truck transporting food from Egypt to Gaza. As the truck passed, an Egyptian vendor tossed more food in. Those small acts show Satya that "other people want to change the world."

She reminds Rishta of other small acts that have changed the world: the trans legislator elected in Northern Virginia, and supportive queer and trans communities they've built around them in their city; the trans person leading the US Department of Health and Human Services; women having the right to vote—and the activists who made that possible. "I feel like there are these little fireflies around us," Satya says, conjuring an image of those few weeks of summer when fireflies light up mountainous forests with their synchronized flashing.

"But how are these fireflies going to merge together to make a big ball of light?" Rishta objects.

Satya turns their disagreement back to her own mental health struggles as a young queer person. "I am really glad I'm alive to tell this story. I have gone through some really dark times where it has felt like it's too hard to go on," she says. "It's my obligation and responsibility to tell people that we have to find some little fireflies."

Rishta does express some joy in her friends and family, and especially her dog—a little brown fluffball named Coco who barks and plays incessantly during our interview.

"Coco is identified as a dog and uses any pronouns because he can't speak," Rishta says, snuggling with the dog. In their most difficult moments navigating the bullying they experienced at school, Rishta says that "Coco was the only one who really understood." She gives the dog a few pets and smiles, before laughing and turning to her mom. "And *you*," Rishta adds, half-teasing, half-earnest.

•

In April 2024, LJ received a message saying that Aaren had used the word "sex" at school—and that LJ ought to know about it.

Aaren had brought a book to school called *I Am Pusheen the Cat* by Claire Belton. The book is about a cute cartoon cat named Pusheen, and on the back of the book, some of Pusheen's characteristics are listed—name, birthday, hobbies, her favorite word ("meow"), as well as Pusheen's dream: "To make friends all over the world."

The book also lists Pusheen's sex ("female").

"It didn't list Pusheen's pronouns," LJ says with a laugh.

Aaren's teacher contacted LJ to let her know that some of Aaren's classmates had been talking about the word "sex"—and traced it back to Aaren. LJ asked Aaren about this. "Where does it say 'sex' in the book?" LJ asked. "And then I was like, right, as a biological term. I asked my kid, "How did you feel when this happened?' And my kid was like . . . 'I felt embarrassed because I had to put my book away.'" LJ says they can hold space in this political climate for the teacher—who may have been afraid of repercussions in what LJ calls a "tar-and-feather" environment. But they also want to find a way forward. "Let's see how we can both learn here and find a solution that's just," she says.

For now, LJ continues working to find that way forward—in a state where, every day, more policies impacting her child are emerging. LJ doesn't want to move unless they need to. "The only thing that will actually get us to uproot is if my babies can't get the support they need," they share. "This is the new motherland for me and my generation . . . I'm rooted in the folks who suffered to be here. We made a relationship to this land."

In the meantime, LJ and their spouse continue to create spaces where their kids can be themselves, regardless of their gender. "We all got manicures at Christmas, and I was thinking the little boys would get toes, but no, they wanted their fingernails—and they were bright like Christmas colors," LJ says. She was a little apprehensive about how Aaren and his brother's friends would react. "We asked them, and they were like, 'My friends thought it was the coolest.' And that's what they continuously help us heal from—the colonialist norms. They remind us and teach us and guide us and show us, and I have no choice but to carry hope."

Chapter Six

On a warm, sunny morning in Flagler County, Florida, in March 2022, about 500 students at Flagler Palm Coast High School walked out of their classrooms and into the school's stadium. They stood on the running track and then climbed up on the bleachers, the grassy football field empty before them. In their hands, they carried bold, colorful signs ("Protect LGBTQ Students" and "Schools Should Be Safe") and waved rainbow flags.

Jack Petocz, an out gay student who helped organize what would become a statewide student walkout, stood a head above the crowd, a megaphone in his hand. If he was nervous, it didn't show. He looked out confidently over the crowd. His black T-shirt read, "The world has bigger problems than boys who kiss boys and girls who kiss girls."

"Stop policing our education!" he shouted into the megaphone. The protesters roared. "How dare Tallahassee ban us from saying gay, from discussing sexual orientation, and coercing staff into outing students!"

Jubilant chants arose from the crowd—"Say gay! Say gay! Say gay!"

That day, students across the state joined Jack and his classmates and walked out of their schools to protest House Bill 1557 (HB 1557). These students knew that, if it passed, HB 1557 would prohibit instruction on sexual orientation and gender identity in kindergarten through third grade.[1] And though "Don't Say Gay" is the informal shorthand for such legislation, civil rights attorney Chase Strangio correctly noted on Twitter (now X) that "The Don't Say Gay Bill is also a Don't Say Trans bill."[2]

Growing up in a conservative household, Jack Petocz hadn't intended to become a youth activist—and certainly not for progressive causes. "I was exposed to Trump rallies every night and extremist radio programs in the car, like Rush Limbaugh," he says. "That was my upbringing."

Around fifth or sixth grade, though, he realized he was queer "and that these kinds of people were trying to actively strip away rights from people like me."

In his junior year of high school, Jack planned his first protest after a school board member filed a police report over the book *All Boys Aren't Blue* in an attempt to remove it from the district's middle and high school libraries. In the memoir, nonbinary writer George M. Johnson recounts their experiences growing up as a young, Black, queer person in New

Jersey. Jack and a few fellow students planned a rally outside the school board meeting where they were discussing the banning of Johnson's book—and several others (including books about racial justice and sexual violence, such as *Stamped*, *Speak*, and *The Hate U Give*).

Censorship laws and policies that impact students and schools, including Florida's "Don't Say LGBTQ+" law, have swept across the United States—and have typically taken aim at books by and about transgender, gender nonconforming, queer, and/or BIPOC people. Just a sampling of the books featuring trans and gender nonconforming characters and topics that were banned in Florida schools in the past few years include: *Beyond Transgender: Transgender Teens Speak Out* by Susan Kuklin; *I Am Jazz* by Jazz Jennings; *The Trans Teen Survival Guide* by Owl Fisher; *Tomboy* by Liz Prince; and *When Aidan Became a Brother* by Kyle Lukoff and Kaylani Juanita.[3]

While schools and libraries are impacted by laws at the state level, book bans are often local, emerging from school boards, district policies, and individual (or coordinated) efforts. (For example, in Florida, during the 2022–2023 school year, almost half the districts in the state—thirty-three out of sixty-nine—had book bans.[4]) Many of the bans are linked to concerted efforts by conservative groups to remove LGBTQ+ and BIPOC stories from library bookshelves:[5] The American Library Association reported in 2023 that more than 4,240 books faced challenges in schools and libraries—far exceeding the previous record high of 2,571 in 2022. Among the titles targeted in 2023, 47 percent represented "the voices and lived experiences of LGBTQIA+ and BIPOC individuals."[6] Florida was only one of many states where libraries and schools experienced attempted (or successful) book bans: from July to December 2023 alone, there were instances of book bans in 23 different states.[7]

In Flagler County, Jack expected only a few dozen students to attend the protest about the district's attempted book ban. When he got to the school board meeting, however, he was surprised to find not only a handful of fellow protestors, but also a crowd of counterprotestors in military gear and body armor. "We had Three Percenters there. We had Proud Boys," he says, referring to two violent extremist, white supremacist groups.[8,9] "We had individuals come from as far as Virginia . . . to a simple protest against book banning."

At the protest, Jack and his teenage friends were called every slur under the sun. The F-word. Abominations. Grown men yelled "horrific racial slurs" at Jack's BIPOC friends. Someone threatened to sexually assault one of the protesters. Later, some counter-protesters tried to follow Jack and his fellow protestors to their cars.

Driving home that night, Jack was shaken. He circled his street three times with his headlights off, afraid he might have been followed. "It was a really scary moment," he remembers.

"But what inadvertently ended up happening was that we were able to reveal that kind of hatred and to expose the kind of people who support book bans."

•

"So many queer people of color who are on the younger side, like my generation—even some people I know who are still in high school or middle school—are like, 'I have so much to say, but no one to listen,'" says Jaiden Blancaflor, a college student and activist living in Ohio. "And that's really the problem."

Jaiden's activism lives at the intersection of disability, LGBTQ+, and racial justice—which reflect his own identities as a disabled, bisexual, trans man who is also a person of color (his parents are Filipino and Salvadoran, respectively). In December 2023, Jaiden wrapped up the second year of a two-year GLSEN Freedom Fellowship, where he worked to make schools safer places for LGBTQ+ students. GLSEN is a longstanding national nonprofit that "champion[s] LGBTQ issues in K–12 education."[10] Jaiden says that a lot of his work centers on highlighting the perspectives of LGBTQ+ people with disabilities—including advocating within GLSEN for closed captioning on all videos and visual descriptions on social media sites like Instagram. "I'm a very strong believer that when you walk into an advocacy space, you're not just advocating for one part of you," he says. "There is no time that a queer person of color can walk into a space and only advocate for this part of them that is queer or that part of them that is a person of color. Because all those systems of oppression are integrated."

Jaiden engaged in online activism—mostly on Instagram—as a young queer and nonbinary teen in the mid-2010s. By 2021, in high school, he was organizing an online transgender prom and was a member of the GLSEN National Student Council.

Jaiden grew up in California, and a lot of the students around him didn't understand—or had misconceptions about—queer identities. For a while, it felt like he was living two different lives—online, he was connected to hundreds of other LGBTQ+ people who helped him feel like he belonged and offered him spaces to lead, speak up, and speak out. But at school and at home, he felt like he had to make himself "as respectable and as consumable as possible."

"Throughout high school, I stuck with a pretty feminine-looking appearance because that was what was safest for me at the time," he says. Even though, internally, he felt more comfortable being masculine, "it was more dangerous to have to explain to people than it was for me to just live with [a feminine appearance]."

As an added complication, he had initially come out as queer and nonbinary—but as he got older, he realized he was a trans man. "I chose at a pretty young age to publicize [my nonbinary identity] online very, very openly," he says. "A big part of [my journey] has been my struggle to allow myself to change and exist without the restrictions of the labels [I used] when I initially came out."

When Jaiden left for college in Ohio in 2021, he came out as a trans man, got a new username on Instagram, and stepped down from leading an online nonbinary organizing space. In the nonvirtual world, he socially and physically transitioned—all while living in a gender-affirming dorm with other trans and gender nonconforming students.

Still, he felt isolated—especially as it was the first year of in-person classes and activities since COVID-19. As a result, a lot of his community continued to be online. The following year, however, Jaiden joined a *Dungeons and Dragons* group that met regularly. "I made friends. But I also know that so many people on campus never had that chance. There are still trans people sitting in a single dorm room by themselves without any friends and not knowing what to do with themselves." Jaiden adds that, "The university does its best to provide things, but they don't want to talk about [trans and queer stuff]. And because they don't want to talk about it, how are people supposed to know about it?"

•

A few months after the school board protest, HB 1557, the Parental Rights in Education Act, passed in the Florida House of Representatives on February 24, 2022. Jack knew he had to do something. So, he made a graphic and posted the following message on Twitter: "Today, the Florida House passed the 'Don't Say Gay' bill. Students are angry, frustrated, and ready to fight this sickening piece of legislation. I'm organizing a statewide school walkout on March 3rd at 12:00 PM in opposition. I encourage student leaders to join me."[11]

Jack thought that only a few area schools would get involved, but before he knew it, his inbox was flooded with messages. Soon, he was helping to organize a mass day of action.

The morning of the walkouts, Jack brought a box of rainbow flags, but the school principal said he couldn't pass them out, telling Jack they were "a political statement" and that he would be violating district procedure if he distributed them. Jack ignored the principal's warning, gathering his friends and handing out fistfuls of flags.

As he left for the walkout, Jack anticipated that only a few others might join him—but instead, hundreds of students from his school did—as well as "tens of thousands of kids" from around the state. From Tampa to Orlando to St. Petersburg, students left their classrooms to protest the unjust bill. With rainbow and trans flags waving and signs in hand, they gathered in front of schools, near football fields, and in courtyards. They spoke and told their stories and chanted.[12]

Ultimately, HB 1557 was signed into law. And even though the demonstration at Flagler Palm Coast High School was initially approved by the school's administration, Jack was subsequently suspended for the actions. He says that the administration kept "repeatedly asking me to temper back the action or to cancel the action"—in his opinion, to limit its success. The walkouts made international news, though, and eventually, the school was pressured to allow Jack to return.

Since the "Don't Say LGBTQ+" walkouts in early March 2022, similar demonstrations have occurred throughout the United States—including a nationwide walkout just a few days after the Florida protests, co-organized by the student-led group Queer Youth Assemble. In addition, 12,000 students staged walkouts across Virginia in September 2022 in protest of Governor Glenn Youngkin's anti-transgender policies, and similar student-led protests have been held in Utah, Texas, and South Dakota.[13]

In Flagler County, Jack's friend and co-organizer Cameron Driggers says that even though HB 1557 passed, the momentum built by the walkout helped them organize students to replace two conservative school board members with LGBTQ+ allies in the next school board election. "The whole state has been written off, especially rural conservative parts," Cameron says. "We think that students have the power to make change themselves. They just need the guidance and the resources to do so."

•

Esmée Silverman, who uses they/she pronouns, said that joining the Gender-Sexuality Alliance (GSA) club in their first year of high school in Massachusetts "kickstarted everything."

At that time, Esmée was struggling with depression, anxiety, and what she later understood to be gender dysphoria. "I really did not want to be alive," she recalls. "So, I had to find something that would keep me tethered to this universe."

Esmée has had queer and trans friends since she was in middle school and felt drawn to her school's GSA. Once she joined, Esmée immediately felt at home. She met people who looked like her and talked like her—and were going through some of the same struggles she was.

Eventually, Esmée went to a regional GSA meeting, where she found herself surrounded by both the warmth of the other participants and their passion for making change. "I immediately knew that this was the work I wanted to do for the rest of my life," they share.

But then the COVID-19 pandemic happened. Now a GSA leader, Esmée moved their club's activities online. This increased community outreach in some regards, as people with disabilities, transportation barriers, or social anxiety now had easier access. Despite this, LGBTQ+ youth experienced a great deal of social isolation during the pandemic. Social supports crumbled, GSA membership plummeted, and "some of those supportive spaces were not coming back."

So, in collaboration with other LGBTQ+ youth, Esmée founded Queer Youth Assemble. "We assemble, build movements, and create awesome, fun events," Esmée says of the group. From ice skating to a pen pal program to organizing protests (for trans athletes, access to healthcare for trans youth, and more) in states across the country, Queer Youth Assemble works to "bring safety, autonomy, and joy to all queer and trans youth under twenty-five in the United States and its territories."[14] The advocacy actions that Queer Youth Assemble engages in are personal to Esmée, as they were a student athlete and also medically transitioned in high school.

Esmée came out as trans—to herself and her loved ones—during her freshman year. "I immediately had a breakdown because I realized how hard it was going to be for the next several years with all of the discrimination," she says. In their junior year of high school, they started taking hormones. However, it wasn't just like they just snapped their fingers and got a prescription. "Much like any medical intervention, there are standards that need to be met," Esmée explains. They saw therapists and doctors and were eventually diagnosed with gender dysphoria. They were then "meticulously" tested and observed by medical and mental health professionals for a year before being prescribed estrogen. "If I didn't have hormones, I would be dead," she says frankly. "I probably would have died by suicide. Because that is the burden that gender dysphoria placed on me." She sighs. "I don't think anybody who supports anti-trans bills has ever gone through that feeling before."

Esmée grew up in a blue state and lives in one now. And

while she's grateful for the protection that offers, she believes "it is not a safe world out there for trans people." She and her friends have had slurs hurled at them, and the day before our interview, she was approached by someone wielding a knife. Luckily, she was able to get away safely.

"There is no immunity anywhere you go," she says.

•

In response to the waves of conservative legislation emanating from the Florida legislature, Cameron and Jack co-founded Youth Action Fund in the summer of 2023. The organization is entirely run by Gen Z college students and supports youth activists in Florida. Local young people come to the organization with an idea, and the Youth Action Fund team provides them with the support they need to help make that idea a reality, from technical assistance to training to funds. Inspired by the ACT UP movement of the 1980s and 1990s, which grew out of the AIDS crisis, Youth Action Fund has helped high schoolers in Orange County register students to vote. They've also supported climate actions and organized an action against book bans.

In early 2024, along with several other organizations in the state, Youth Action Fund helped coordinate a "die-in" at the Florida Department of Motor Vehicles locations in Orlando, Miami, Tampa, and Gainesville. The action—which drew 200 participants—protested a new statewide policy that prevents transgender Floridians from changing their gender markers on their driver's licenses. Each die-in lasted thirty-seven minutes—a nod to the 37 percent of transgender Floridians who say they experience harassment and discrimination due to inaccurate IDs.[15]

While the activist work he engages in is difficult, Jack is tired of hearing that trans and queer Floridians should just give up and leave the state. "I think we need to recognize that the right—the ability—to leave is a privilege. I come from a low-income background. A lot of trans and queer people do not have the monetary resources to leave Florida," Jack says. "I don't need to be told that I need to leave my home. I need to be supported . . . so we don't just write off an entire state."

•

As queer and trans youth activists keep working to make the world—and their states—more loving and more affirming, Jaiden offers one piece of advice: pace yourself. Jaiden has faced backlash for stepping back on occasion, with people telling him, "You don't care as much as you used to."

"It's not that I don't care as much as I used to," he says in response. "It's that a movement can't move . . . if the individual people cannot move."

At the same time, he emphasizes that LGBTQ+ youth need

support—from adults and other young people—more than ever. “It’s important to change the systems for future generations, but it’s also important to acknowledge the generations that are here, alive, present. It’s not enough to say, ‘Oh, we’re working on it. We’re lobbying [against] these laws. We’re doing this. We’re doing that. We’re doing all this background work that will make change in twenty years’ time,’” he says. “We need events now. We need connection now.”

Esmée makes it abundantly clear that the community she built with her GSA saved her life. And if it weren’t for the books she read about queer and trans identities and the care she’s received from her medical team, she wouldn’t be who she is today. As a result, she keeps working to make those types of connections for others. In early 2024, Esmée told us that they want to mobilize LGBTQ+ communities across the United States on October 11, which is National Coming Out Day, “to encourage people to come out (if it is safe for them to do so) and advocate for a unified community that can support itself regardless of the 2024 election.” They hope that after this event, “every single person in this country will know at least one queer or trans person by the time the election comes around.” Esmée’s philosophy is that “if people just see us, if people just meet us, if people just know us, then that creates a huge change in their attitude towards trans people.”

Knowing other queer and trans people has been a literal lifeline for Jack.

During our interview in early 2024, he says he recently tested positive for COVID-19. He also shares that he had just been kicked out of his family's house—when he had a 103-degree fever. "The trans die-in was the final straw for them," he says.

After his family threw him out, Jack didn't know what to do next. "I didn't have anywhere to go, and I just told close friends what happened and told the space that we built online. And now I'm safe and sound in an Airbnb because of the community that we built," he says. "It's so meaningful for me in this moment. And it truly proves that when you build community and chosen family . . ."

He trails off.

"We look out for each other, you know?"

Chapter Seven

Eli Bundy didn't know what to expect when he walked into the Equality Hub in North Charleston, South Carolina, on a Tuesday night in November 2019. His mom had encouraged him to attend a community meeting called "What's at Stake for LGBTQ Youth" organized by local and national LGBTQ+ advocacy organizations. While Eli wasn't sure what would happen at the meeting, he was curious about queer politics and was eager to meet others in his city with similar interests.

A few dozen people, mostly adults aside from the fourteen-year-old Eli, sat in a circle of chairs, group therapy-style, snacking on veggies and dip, while a few special guests shared information about a range of LGBTQ+-themed topics. Eli listened to information about the *Bostock v. Clayton County* employment discrimination case that had recently been heard by the US Supreme Court, as well as a discussion about a local school board's exclusionary anti-transgender policy on student records. Then Julie Wilensky, an attorney from the

National Center for Lesbian Rights (NCLR), spoke about South Carolina's 1988 Comprehensive Health Education Act, which had a provision colloquially known as the "No Promo Homo" clause. The clause prohibited South Carolina schools from including any information about non-heterosexual relationships in its health or sex education curriculum, unless the information was shared in the context of sexually transmitted infections.[1]

Eli's ears perked up: he remembered back in eighth grade in health class when a friend asked a question about a same-sex relationship. "We can't really talk about that," the instructor had responded. Eli, who identified as queer, had been frustrated by this. What was so wrong with talking about LGBTQ+ relationships?

Something clicked. "I had assumed that my teacher was just being difficult—like they didn't want to talk about it because they personally had some sort of opposition to talking about queer sex ed," Eli recalls. "But actually, it wasn't that: they were prevented by this law—and maybe that teacher was actually cool but was being prevented by the state from being cool."

Eli approached Julie after the event. "I want to help with this," he told her, giving her his email to keep in touch. "I experienced this firsthand, and I want to make sure it doesn't happen again."

A few weeks later, Julie called and asked Eli if he thought his school's Gender and Sexualities Alliance (GSA) might be interested in being a plaintiff in a legal challenge to the "No Promo Homo" law.[2] Eli was in.

His experience in health class wasn't the first time that Eli felt that talking about LGBTQ+ issues was off-limits at his school. In the seventh grade, he wanted to start a GSA, so he approached a trusted teacher to ask if she'd be the advisor, a requirement for a new school club. He remembers her immediately becoming chilly toward him, saying that she was already the advisor for a student organization dedicated to supporting Christian student artists—and that advising both clubs would be a "conflict of interest." At the time, Eli was confused about what she meant, until later that year when he tried to bond with her in outrage over a form letter he received from South Carolina's US Senator Tim Scott that expressed opposition to the freedom to marry for same-gender couples. The teacher defended Tim Scott and his positions. "I think I just, like, misread this teacher," Eli remembers, cringing.

Another student was able to later start a GSA at the high school, but when they graduated and no one picked up the mantle, Eli stepped in to lead. "For a while, I sort of operated it as almost an illicit school club," Eli says. "I was scared of that previous experience of being summarily rejected by a potential advisor."

One of Eli's first ideas for the club was challenging the "No Promo Homo" policy. He wanted to bring Julie into a virtual meeting as a guest speaker to talk about what might be possible—but once again he was met with opposition. The faculty sponsor said that advising a club focusing on a political issue like this might compromise their job, while an administrator said that Eli personally risked "disciplinary action" from the school district if the GSA challenged South Carolina's Department of Education.

Eli found this not only shocking—the school, after all, was a public magnet high school specializing in arts and music—but also scary. "My siblings also went to school there, and it just made me think: if I get kicked out, my siblings are going to be, like, the siblings of the guy who got kicked out of school!" Eli consulted with his parents and endured meeting after meeting with the school administration; eventually, they backpedaled and told him that legally they could not stop the GSA from meeting with a guest speaker or discussing the lawsuit.

The members of the GSA spoke about their options online, at lunch, and during their GSA meetings—but in the hallway, because Eli was worried about putting the club's advisor into a tense situation with the administration. They eventually decided to move forward and participate in a lawsuit: Eli would go public and share his story on behalf of the group, but no one else from the club would have to be publicly associated with the case.

NCLR, in partnership with Lambda Legal, SC Equality, and the Campaign for Southern Equality, filed the lawsuit in February 2020, fully preparing for the complaint to be the opening salvo in a years-long process to dismantle the antiquated anti-LGBTQ+ policy. The case made big news, and Eli spoke with reporters from across the country, including high-profile outlets like National Public Radio and NBC News.

Then, just two weeks later, a delightful surprise: officials in South Carolina agreed that the law was unconstitutional, and the court entered a consent decree, blocking the curriculum censorship law from being enforced.[3]

When Julie called to tell Eli the good news, he was surprised, confused, proud, and relieved all at once—surprised because the process had been faster than he ever imagined, confused because he thought the Republican leaders in South Carolina would resist the lawsuit more aggressively, proud to have been a part of taking down a dangerous thirty-two-year-old statewide policy, and relieved that no other student would have to endure the "No Promo Homo" law in South Carolina. "The reason that we wanted to get involved in the first place was our fear of other students enduring the same discrimination, shame, and exclusion that we felt at school," Eli says. "Knowing that no other student in South Carolina will go through their sex education under that mandate was so gratifying."

•

At the time, the "No Promo Homo" victory was the latest in what had largely been an exciting, hopeful few years for the LGBTQ+ movement. Same-gender couples were marrying in every single state, without issue. Transgender students were winning major court cases, including a case filed by Gavin Grimm, a transgender student in Virginia who challenged his school's policies prohibiting him from using the boys' restroom.[4] LGBTQ+ people were also being elected to office in all corners of the country, from Danica Roem in Virginia to Jared Polis in Colorado to Phillippe Cunningham and Andrea Jenkins in Minneapolis, Minnesota. *TIME Magazine* had declared the "Transgender Tipping Point," whatever that meant.[5]

Even bad developments seemed to result in steps forward. For example, North Carolina's 2016 passage of HB 2, the notorious "bathroom ban," provoked massive protests and boycotts against the state, one of the first national uprisings in support of transgender equality.[6] President Trump's attempts to ban open military service for transgender people resulted in prominent Republican senators speaking positively about transgender people for the first time.[7]

And in 2018, when extremist forces tried to roll back protections for transgender people in the first-ever statewide referendum specifically about transgender rights in the United States, voters unequivocally defended transgender equality. That historic campaign in Massachusetts was centered around a law prohibiting discrimination against transgender people in places of public accommodation—businesses, restaurants, parks and public transportation. However, according to the anti-trans side, "public accommodation" only meant one thing: bathrooms.

Anti-equality opponents tried to keep the nondiscrimination bill from passing in the state legislature in 2016, squawking about how the law supposedly put women at risk of violence in the bathroom, and they hustled up enough signatures to get a referendum on the ballot.

But the scare tactics were no match for the "Yes on 3" coalition—or for the many transgender youth whose stories were at the heart of the effort to protect them from discrimination.

One of these young people was Ashton, who spent much of his time in eighth and ninth grades fighting to defend the nondiscrimination law. "It was like we had no choice but to use our voice and speak up, because discrimination was something that I could face when I opened the front door, when I got to school, when I was out at the movie theater with friends," Ashton remembers. "This was very real."

He and his mother Carmen showed up wherever they could—to meet with legislators and speak at campaign events. They even went door-to-door, canvassing voters. "Being a person of color, I wanted to make sure that we were reaching out to Black communities, Spanish-speaking communities, Hispanic communities," Ashton says. He identifies as Black and Afro-Latino, and he and his mom speak Spanish, which came in handy during the "get out the vote" efforts.

One day in the spring of 2018, Ashton and Carmen knocked on a door just a few streets down from where they lived in Lowell. An older, Spanish-speaking man greeted them, and it became clear that he hadn't given much thought to transgender people and wasn't familiar with the ballot question. "To see how accepting he was, and how he began to understand, it felt like there was this gap of knowledge that could easily be filled with just a small amount of communication," Ashton recalls. "I saw the full effects of storytelling, right in front of me."

Going door-to-door, Carmen shares, "allowed folks to connect as humans. It wasn't even an LGBTQ thing. It was more trying to connect as humans, as parents, as people who want to support their family. And the fact that we're different shouldn't stop that connection. A lot of people were like, 'Of course you deserve to feel that your son is safe, of course your child deserves to be loved and respected and supported.' I talked about unconditional love and faith and what my role as a parent was. My role was to love unconditionally, and that to me is the work of God."

Another young person who became vital to the success of the Yes on 3 campaign was Nicole Talbot. In 2015, when Nicole was fourteen, her mom Jeanne testified before the Massachusetts Joint Committee on the Judiciary in support of the nondiscrimination law. She brought with her a three-foot-tall photo of Nicole, smiling and wearing a red jacket. "Our work is not done until my daughter Nicole is protected under the law just like any other fourteen-year-old girl in the state of Massachusetts," she said.[8]

Nicole, Ashton, and other young people became the faces of the Yes on 3 campaign. Massachusetts residents heard from them again and again in news articles and television spots, and the campaign put out social media graphics that featured their stories and images. "There's something unique about transgender youth," Nicole says, reflecting on the campaign and the impact that youth can have on people's hearts and minds. "When these people were meeting me, they saw their children and grandchildren. It was interesting to see people change their opinions."

At the community watch party in Boston on election night 2018, Nicole, Ashton, and their moms gathered with advocates from across the state who had worked so hard to protect transgender dignity—and they soon found out that they had a lot to celebrate. Once all the votes were counted, 67.8 percent of voters selected "Yes," protecting the transgender-inclusive nondiscrimination law.[9] "Once we hit that 60 percent, we were like, we got it," Nicole says. "Everyone was yelling and screaming, and everyone started having champagne, with all the kids like us in the corner hanging out. It felt like we were making history, and that was really special to be a part of. It helped build up my self-confidence as a person—it felt like, 'Yes, we are doing this. We are changing the world.'"

While Ashton was also thrilled about the results, they also gave him pause. "We won by a two-to-one margin," he says. "But my mind also went to, 'Wow, 33 percent of Massachusetts does not support transgender people like me being safe from discrimination.' And what would happen if there were similar efforts in states like Kansas or Oklahoma, where they have more hostile anti-LGBTQ attitudes? It made me think about what we could do in Massachusetts to continue the fight—because, even just thinking about myself, what will my rights look like the minute I cross the state border? Or what about my friends who live in red states where legislation is really intense? So I think it was a bittersweet moment—in Massachusetts, we had a big win, but we're just one of fifty states."

•

One of those other fifty states was South Carolina. And despite the victory in the "No Promo Homo" case, the state was not immune to a new variety of anti-LGBTQ+ legislation—legislation that shined a harsh spotlight directly onto transgender young people.

The COVID-19 pandemic and stay-at-home orders derailed much of the legislative work across the country in 2020, resulting in little movement for anti-transgender laws (except for Idaho, where lawmakers found time amid the most significant social and economic upheaval in a generation to pass a law banning transgender kids from playing school sports). However, anti-LGBTQ+ legislation roared back with a vengeance in 2021.

Eli Bundy, whose first foray into LGBTQ+ political activism had been an unbridled success, jumped into action. Over the course of 2021, he became more confident in his trans identity as a nonbinary person (at the time, he used they/them pronouns), and he knew how important it was that South Carolina lawmakers heard from trans and queer youth directly on legislation that would impact them.

On a chilly day in February 2021, he left his eleventh-grade classroom and patiently spent over two hours in the teacher's lounge, awaiting his turn to deliver virtual testimony opposing an anti-trans sports ban before a South Carolina House subcommittee. The hearing concluded without the bill moving forward (although it advanced the following week).

Later in the legislative session, Eli was a part of a group of students who had a virtual meeting with Representative Ashley Trantham, the South Carolina lawmaker who had proposed the bill—despite her saying that she did not know of a single transgender student in South Carolina who was participating in school sports. The meeting felt hopeful at first—but that hope quickly turned to frustration.

One student talked about how there were many reasons why student athletes can have a competitive advantage—for example, by being particularly tall or having longer-than-average legs. The student explained that it would be heartbreaking for them if they weren't able to run track just because they were too tall—so why should students be singled out because they were transgender?

Trantham put on a sympathetic voice: "If you were my kid and somebody tried to stop you from running track for being too tall, I would go to war for you."

"I remember thinking, 'You're on the other side!'" Eli recalls. "You're saying that you're going to go to war for this kid in this hypothetical world where he can't run because he's too tall, but at the same time you're going after trans kids who are trying to play sports—probably *badly*—for their high school league? Are you serious?"

There were other major fumbles during the meeting—Trantham misgendered several participants, and at one point, she dug her heels in, saying that all she was trying to do was protect women's sports. "I really thought that maybe the problem was that she didn't know any trans people. Maybe she thought we were scary boogeymen who hid in your closet, and maybe if she actually talked to us she would realize we're quite nice," Eli says. "And we were *so nice* on that call! We really did a great job and represented trans youth in South Carolina really well. I felt like we crushed it! And I thought that when she looked trans people in the face, she would realize that these are kids, and she's harassing and aggravating kids unnecessarily. But she *did not care*—like, at all."

"You want politics to work the way it's supposed to work, and for the constituency of the legislators to determine how the legislator votes—but obviously that's not the way it actually works," he continues. "That meeting really changed a lot about how I thought about this. I saw that it's not that they don't know trans people—it's that they don't *care* about trans people, and they're just using trans people as a wedge issue."

Eli wound up breaking down on the call with Trantham, as well as in a debriefing space (without the representative there) held afterward. "I was sobbing," he says. "Sobbing on Zoom is the worst."

•

One thing that Nicole, Ashton, and Eli all share is that they were sure of their gender identity from a young age.

Ashton came out to his parents on his twelfth birthday. He thought at the time, "If I come out on my birthday, there's no way they can get mad."

Eli wrote a letter to his parents at eleven saying that he was bisexual and shortly after came out to friends as genderqueer. In the sixth grade, he started going by his middle name. "I knew something needed to change," he remembers. "That was a step in the right direction, but I couldn't quite place that it was a gender thing." By the end of that year, he knew he wanted to use they/them pronouns, and in conversations with friends, he felt like he was doing a "perpetual Reddit AMA [Ask Me Anything]" about the LGBTQ+ community. The final straw that pushed him to come out to his parents as trans happened in seventh grade when he wanted to wear a tuxedo to his band concert instead of a dress. "I told them, 'I want to be a boy'—but that wasn't really true. It's not that I *wanted* to be a boy; it's that I wasn't a girl."

For Nicole, her gender was a long-running conversation in her household. "My trains had tea parties, and I loved *Mulan*," she says, referencing the Disney movie featuring a woman who poses as a man. "My mom tried to dress me in gender-neutral Halloween costumes, and I ended up trading costumes with friends in kindergarten and dressing in the parade as a princess." Nicole's mom Jeanne created a safe space at home, allowing Nicole to wear dresses and pink flip-flops, play with Barbies, and live as a girl. Jeanne also signed Nicole up for a weekend-long family camp in fifth grade alongside other families with gender nonconforming children—but the gender exploration otherwise didn't really leave the home. Jeanne read a lot about transgender people's experiences in the United States, and back in the early 2010s, there weren't many positive stories.

It was a totally different situation with Nicole's dad—her parents had been divorced since she was two years old, but early custody was shared. He was not at all affirming. "Even wearing a boy's pink bathing suit was not okay," Nicole recalls. "Having my toenails painted was not okay. Having my hair longer was not okay." When Nicole played Gavroche in a production of *Les Miserábles*, she grew out her hair. "The night the show ended, he took me into the bathroom, pinned me to the wall, and shaved my head. It really solidified for me that, to him, I wasn't allowed to be anything but his son."

"It was a constant battle between who I was trying to become and who I was allowed to be," she adds. She describes it as living three separate lives—as Nicole at home; as a flamboyant and feminine boy at school with her deadname (the name a transgender person was given at birth but no longer uses[10]); and striving to live as the perfect son with her father. "It was a lot of juggling those three worlds and those three separate identities."

Her father ultimately became a Jehovah's Witness, and at thirteen, Nicole chose to stop speaking to or seeing him. "I realized it was harder to hold on than to let go," she says.

Nicole then began exploring her medical transition. After performing female roles in her school plays and musicals, thrilled to finally express her correct gender, Nicole desperately wanted to ensure that her voice would not change as puberty approached. She had long been seeing a therapist and counselor, but at thirteen she began going to a gender clinic in Boston. There were many steps in the year-long transitioning process, including seemingly endless paperwork, phone calls, emails, evaluations, blood tests, and many visits to the clinic.

In the meantime, Nicole experienced a happy period of acceptance at school. She attended a school in Beverly, Massachusetts, that specialized in youth with language-based learning disabilities (Nicole has dyslexia), and in the middle of seventh grade, she worked with her school principal to formally announce her identity to her classmates and share some educational materials with them. The school hosted an assembly where they spoke openly about gender identity, and they encouraged an open dialogue between Nicole and the other students.

"It was amazing," Nicole says. "A lot of people who bullied me seemed to understand more. They were like, 'This makes so much sense now, and I'm so sorry for all that I did.'"

"There's this assumption that children don't know what's happening, but especially right now, kids already have access to this information—these conversations are already happening," Nicole continues. "Kids are able to have these adult conversations and handle these concepts when they're talked about in a way that's constructive and educational. I was the first in my community to come out and share my story—and that was helpful when the next trans person came out. The way my school handled it set that expectation of light, love, and acceptance no matter who you are."

•

After the Massachusetts ballot campaign, Ashton became a Youth Ambassador for the Human Rights Campaign (HRC), which required a great deal of public speaking on his part about being a transgender young person. "I didn't really understand the magnitude of it at the time," he says. "But I dove in headfirst, shifting from state or local organizing to this large national platform. The advocacy work that I had been doing in Massachusetts was a necessity—but later it became a passion. I would read a headline about something LGBTQ-related and want to get involved."

He shared his story at a national HRC conference, spoke to educators and journalists and professionals, and became a Champion with The GenderCool Project. Through GenderCool, Ashton co-authored a children's book called *A Kids Book About Being Inclusive*, one in a series of similar books for kids.[11] "It was amazing to hold that book in my hands and know that this was something that young LGBTQ+ kids and their friends could read."

In June 2021, as a sophomore in high school, Ashton was invited to introduce President Joe Biden at the White House's Pride reception. He brought a copy of his book and hand-delivered it to President Biden and the First Lady, Dr. Jill Biden. "That was amazing," Ashton says. "It was an honor to be able to give those and be acknowledged not only as a young person who wrote a book but also as an Afro-Latino transgender person literally standing in the White House in front of the president and his wife, sharing this set of books. In a lot of ways it was, like, 'Wow—look at where we are, and look at where my advocacy journey has brought me in this moment.'"

•

Nicole's advocacy for transgender equality in her early college years quickly became very personal. "There's this assumption that states like Massachusetts are always safe," she explains. "But that's not been my experience. Even though Massachusetts has protective laws, I'm finding that people who want to hate or fear transgender people, no matter where they are, will find a way to do that. People often say, 'You live in Massachusetts, everything's fine.' But it's not always that way. Anti-transgender sentiment is sweeping the country."

After graduating high school, Nicole began pursuing a Bachelor of Arts in musical theater at an acclaimed conservatory in Boston. However, it wasn't long before she felt unwelcome and rejected by the program and her peers. Beyond issues that run deep in musical theater and performance spaces, such as unhealthy conversations about how students' bodies are supposed to look, Nicole grappled with conversations from a teacher that definitely crossed a line. He told her, essentially, that she needed to stop bringing gender identity into the classroom and into her performances: "He wanted me to just be, like, Nicole the cis woman because, he said, I did a good job of acting like one." The teacher later made comments about Nicole's body, assuming that she had had many surgeries related to her gender identity.

When Nicole posted about her experience on social media,

she didn't receive much support from her peers and classmates. The whole environment, she says, was toxic and unhealthy. Nicole left the theater program halfway through her degree. "For a long time, my mental health and physical health were not in a good place," she says.

On top of that, around the same time, she was featured in a news story in *The New York Times Magazine*.[12] The landlord of her Boston apartment saw it and learned for the first time that Nicole is transgender. Shortly after, when it came time to renew Nicole's lease, he refused. And while discrimination is challenging to prove, Nicole feels certain that it was related to her transgender identity.

All these disappointments came against the backdrop of state after state passing laws that targeted transgender people. Many of the laws directly impacted friends that Nicole had made in her journey as an advocate, including Ashton. "For a lot of the last two years, I've been trying to keep my head in the sand, kind of turning inwards and focusing on my own self-healing," she says. "Part of me feels kind of guilty about it—and not being at the forefront of all of the fighting against these bills as I've done in the past. But I've been trying to focus on healing myself and rebuilding."

•

Eli took a year off between high school and college. Part of that was so that he could use the gap year to explore a bit more of the country and things he liked to do, especially rock climbing and learning how to sail. But he also wanted to adjust to a medical transition before going to college. While he thought about starting hormone therapy at sixteen, he and his parents had an agreement that he'd wait until after high school.

Eli had top surgery in March 2023. (For transmasculine people, top surgery typically involves removing chest tissue to create a more masculine appearance.[13]) Two weeks later, while he was recovering at home, he hitched a ride with friends to the state capital, Columbia, to join with other South Carolinians who were fighting against a ban on gender-affirming care for transgender youth.

A few days after the event in Columbia, Eli began taking testosterone. And later that summer, he started at Bowdoin College in Maine. The change, he says, has been unbelievably powerful. "In some ways, it breaks my heart that I left South Carolina," he shares. "I feel like I quit on people—on all of the people who come out to the statehouse and testify against bad legislation."

Still, he was excited for his next steps. He joined the choir at Bowdoin—he now likes the way his voice sounds. He also got involved in the school's queer and trans community, working for the Sexuality, Women and Gender Center (SWAG, "the coolest acronym," he laughs), coordinating events, and supporting Gender Matters, an LGBTQ+ student group on campus.

He feels accepted and comfortable being himself, especially while doing outdoor adventure activities like swimming and canoeing. "My homeostasis, average, normal day is just a *lot* better," he says. "My base level of how I'm doing as a person is just ridiculously improved."

He is also making friends. "Before I started transitioning, I would meet people and feel like they were sort of meeting a prototype," he says. "I hoped at the time that they were meeting a version of me that they wouldn't know forever. But now I'm like, 'Actually, this is kind of, like, *who I am*. Yeah—now, it's correct.'"

His message for other trans people is simple in theory but complicated in practice: try to ignore the naysayers and instead dream big about what's possible. "I did not have a single positive force in my life who was like, 'Maybe transitioning would be good.' And there was a lot of political noise that it would be really bad," he says. "I kind of wish that I'd had somebody in my life who said, 'You don't have to transition—but if you do, I really think it might all turn out great and be helpful and improve your life.' Because for me, it's been awesome."

•

For all these young people, the pressure of being teen advocates was very real—but each of them also explains that it has been a critical part of their development.

Ashton drew on anger and frustration as fuel for his advocacy work. "I wasn't fighting because I wanted to fight for our rights every day," he explains. "It's more that I was frustrated and didn't want people to have to go through what I experienced." Still, Ashton says, "I will always be a trans advocate and activist." And his work is intersectional to its core: "I realized early on because of my intersectional identity and experience advocating for the Black community and the Afro-Latino community and just Spanish-speaking spaces, that every marginalized community or group that is being attacked, their battle is my battle, too. Because who's going to show up for me when we need to gather support across the nation for trans people? It's not going to be the people who I didn't show up for. It's going to be the people who I *did* show up for."

"It was life-changing," Nicole says of her advocacy work in Massachusetts. "I wouldn't have had it any other way. I know a lot of trans kids who wanted to help but who didn't want to be seen as trans, or maybe it wasn't safe for them to be out so publicly. But for me, my advocacy allowed me to build my community while I was becoming who I am today. It gave me an outlet to talk about my experience, to talk about who I am, and to grow and mature through that process."

As she reflects on her childhood advocacy, Nicole is also coming to terms with the negative experiences she faced in college. "I've been slowly rebuilding my confidence and my voice," she says. "I was thinking about never singing again. I was thinking about not wanting to even be here anymore. But music got me through all those dark points in my life."

Music has always been a source of comfort and inspiration for Nicole. "It just gives you an escape where you can feel safe, where you can feel protected, where you don't have that pressure from the world around you," she explains. "I hope other kids who are going through hard times find something that gives them joy or passion."

The spring of 2024 marked ten years since the start of Nicole's social and medical transition, and she celebrated the best way a performer like her knows how: by hosting a ten-year anniversary one-woman show that she titled, "Thank Heaven for Little Girls." She invited friends from middle school, high school, and college, folks she had worked with, supportive family members, and even people who were a part of her Yes on 3 journey.

In a gorgeous black dress, Nicole came out on the stage at Club Cafe in Boston and performed a wide-ranging set of songs that spoke to different periods of her life, from her gender identity to challenges with her father. One of the songs she sang, of course, was the highlight of her favorite Disney movie, "Reflection" from *Mulan*.

After she sang the last wistful notes, she looked out across the faces of the crowd and bowed.

They gave her a standing ovation.

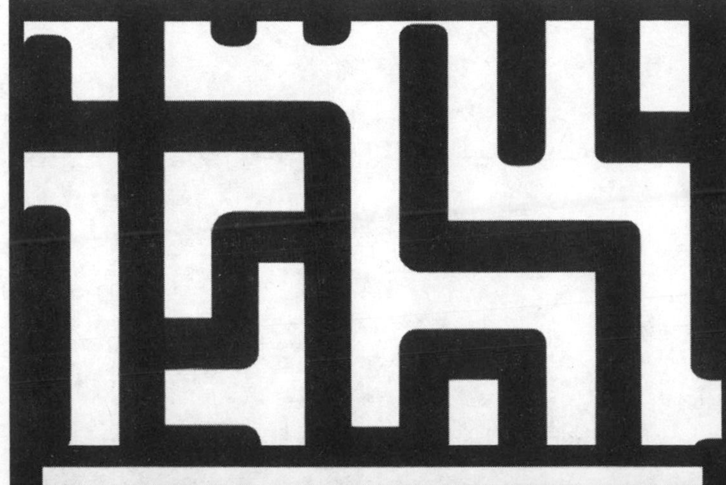

PART III: DON'T GO IT ALONE

Chapter Eight

Dusk was falling in Charleston, South Carolina, as they started filing into Union Station. Some were dressed in glittering gowns, while others wore white button-ups with dark suspenders. The humid coastal breeze wove between them as they walked in pairs or groups or solo toward the nondescript entrance of the stout, white building.

Once they got inside, it was like a world transformed: globes of light hung from the ceiling, and swirling, colorful projections danced along a back wall. Music thumped from large speakers. In the middle of the room, they bounced and swayed to the music—some laughing, some holding hands. Rainbow flags were scattered across the tables. Several of them clutched rainbow fans, waving them with joy.

It was late April 2022, and the occasion was the first queer youth prom hosted in three years by We Are Family, a local LGBTQ+-serving organization. In March 2020, as COVID-19 swept across the United States, We Are Family put its in-person events, activities, and social support groups on hold—including its queer youth prom.

Like many other organizations, We Are Family adapted to the pandemic by moving into virtual spaces, in the process beefing up its mutual aid and launching a Mental Health Assistance Program, which provides free therapy to LGBTQ+ youth in South Carolina. By investing in online spaces, We Are Family was able to reach trans youth throughout the South Carolina Lowcountry (the southeastern coastal region of the state) who might never make it up to Charleston because of transportation issues, not being out to their families, or other barriers. At the same time, though, the youth that We Are Family served—as well as the organization's staff members—greatly missed the in-person connections they had enjoyed before the pandemic.

So, when We Are Family opened the doors for the 2022 Charleston Queer Youth Prom (with the theme "A Garden in Outer Space"), queer and trans joy emanated from every corner of the high-ceilinged ballroom. Almost 250 young people from across the South Carolina Lowcountry came to the prom that night, where attendees were free to be their whole selves—as queer or trans or questioning kids—without anyone policing what they wore, who they danced with, or how they expressed themselves. For many of those present, this was the first time they had experienced an event like that. At their schools, they might not be allowed to bring a same-gender date to the prom—or if they were allowed, they might be bullied or laughed at for being queer or trans. Or their parents might not let them wear a skirt or suit—or a mix of the two—because of how they thought "boys" and "girls" should dress or act.

As the night wore on, several students stepped outside for some air, their prom dresses bright splashes of color against the building's white walls. "I'm glad that there's a place like this where people can come together and truly be who they are," one said, "without people staring or judging them."

Two other high schoolers said they were on a first date, smiles playing across their faces. "Seeing so many people that could relate to me and that could have the same pronouns, same issues—that's queer joy," one of them commented.

Later, as the prom ended and the crowd disbursed, a teenager in glasses sat on a bench, watching their fellow promgoers. In the South, they said, "it almost feels like you need to hide your identity." In school, "queerness is not acknowledged, and it's not respected." But in spaces like this, "there are a lot of us, and we are here to support each other."

•

We Are Family was founded in 1995 by Tom Myers, the father of a gay son. After Tom's son came out, he realized that there was a dearth of resources for LGBTQ+ young people in South Carolina. To remedy this, he wanted to create an organization that could educate the community about LGBTQ+ issues—and show queer and trans youth that there were adults who supported them.

At first, We Are Family sent affirming information and educational materials by mail to community leaders from whom LGBTQ+ youth could seek support. Volunteers also spoke to church congregations and other nonprofit groups. Two years after its launch, We Are Family began facilitating its first support group for queer youth.

Today, We Are Family reaches more than 1,500 LGBTQ+ and allied youth annually. Though they primarily operate in the South Carolina Lowcountry, they have ambitious plans to expand some of their programs statewide, including their Mental Health Assistance Program. From helping students launch and lead Gender-Sexuality Alliances at their local schools to providing leadership development, We Are Family works to equip LGBTQ+ youth with the skills needed for advocacy—and to create safe spaces for them to prosper.

Jonatan Guerrero Ramirez directs We Are Family's events and manages the organization's thrift store, Closet Case. "Growing up, I never saw somebody like myself," Jonatan shares. "I was one of the only Hispanic kids in my school, and I really didn't see myself thriving. I didn't see myself being a successful adult—being a queer, successful Latinx individual."

Jonatan first learned about We Are Family through the thrift store program he now directs. He was studying fashion and design at the Art Institute of Charleston and was assigned a "deconstruction project"—he had to find some clothing, take it apart, and remake it into something new. As he searched the internet for thrift shops, he stumbled upon Closet Case, which didn't have a physical space yet, but held pop-up shops around the city.

As a queer youth and undocumented immigrant growing up in the South, Jonatan was taught not to be too expressive (though he admits that was hard given his outgoing personality). Walking into the Closet Case pop-up store was the first time he saw queer youth and trans folks living their authentic lives.

Shortly after, he signed up as a volunteer with We Are Family. As a senior in college, he helped plan the organization's youth prom. Jonatan was in his early twenties at the time, but he says that "seeing queer kids thrive and be themselves inspired me." Now, as a staff person at We Are Family, he wants to be the kind of resource he needed—but didn't have—when he was a kid.

Jonatan was born in Mexico, but his family immigrated to the United States when he was a child. Growing up, he didn't know the words "gay" or "queer," but he knew he had crushes on other boys. Eventually, he opened up to his friends and parents about his feelings, though he still tried to keep his queerness hidden—along with his immigration status. As a senior in high school, while his peers were applying for college, Jonatan applied for Deferred Action for Childhood Arrivals (DACA), a federal program established by the Obama Administration to protect people who immigrated to the United States as children from deportation and help them get legal work permits. Jonatan was one of the first people to receive DACA after it was launched in June 2012.

It was only after Jonatan joined the staff at We Are Family, though, that he learned to be his whole self. At the conferences he attended, like Creating Change (a national conference for LGBTQ+ advocates and individuals), he admired the immigrant trans women he met who were out-and-proud activists—both as undocumented immigrants and as Brown trans women. When Jonatan returned to Charleston from those meetings, he realized there were eyes on him, too: queer and trans undocumented kids at We Are Family who were looking up to *him* as a Brown, queer immigrant.

It's one of the reasons he decided to open up about his immigration status—and one of the reasons he remains at We Are Family. At first, he says, "I told myself, 'I'll just be here for a couple of years, and I'll move on.'" But he has stuck around so he can "keep empowering these youth, especially our Latinx and undocumented kids who are facing these scary challenges now."

•

Over its nearly three-decade history, We Are Family has

been through a lot of changes. In the last several years, the organization has grown from having one full-time staff member to a staff of six—and has increased its programming to match that growth. It has also shifted from being a White-led organization to being run by a team that is primarily BIPOC and trans and gender nonconforming. From the AIDS crisis to the legalization of same-gender marriage, the organization has persisted through the ups and downs of political seasons—in the heart of the Bible Belt.

"South Carolina is just such a challenging context," explains Domenico Ruggerio, We Are Family's Executive Director, who uses they/he pronouns. In the early 2000s, Domenico helped start a GSA in their high school on Long Island, New York—where they faced their own share of challenges. When Domenico joined We Are Family in 2021, he was surprised to see that those same challenges persisted for LGBTQ+ youth in South Carolina: Principals who didn't want a GSA at their school, or teachers who were afraid of pushback if they were advisors to queer or trans clubs.

When Jonatan started working at We Are Family in the late-2010s, trans youth were mainly testifying against bathroom bills. Today, the organization's staff are dealing with different issues, such as talking about how to help transgender youth who lose access to gender-affirming care or who are "outed" to their parents, having their gender identity or sexual orientation disclosed without their consent. "Kids should be worried about who they're going to prom with," Jonatan says. "Instead of studying for an exam or a state test, they're studying their statements" to testify at the statehouse.

Cora Webb, the organization's Program Director, agrees. "Growing up is hard enough," says Cora, who uses any pronouns. "Remember how hard it was to find jeans that fit? To do your hair?" Along with becoming who you want to be in the world, "imagine all the obstacles that are added on if you're queer or you're trans. When you see it as a blessing, but other people see it as a curse."

We Are Family has been part of several successful efforts for social and policy change in South Carolina. In 2020, they supported the effort detailed in chapter seven to overturn the state's more than thirty-year-old "No Promo Homo" law. That same year, they worked with the Charleston County School District's (CCSD) Health Advisory committee and local organizations like Carolina Youth Action Project and Women's Rights Empowerment Network to push for comprehensive sex education in CCSD schools. Ultimately, the school board approved an LGBTQ+-inclusive comprehensive sex ed curriculum.[1] And as anti-LGBTQ+ laws and policies have arisen across the state and region, We Are Family has mobilized and organized LGBTQ+ youth to speak out in protest.

According to Domenico, the political attacks that LGBTQ+ youth are facing today—at all levels, from the state government to school districts—are creating a sense of urgency and fear. "Our youth are definitely feeling that they are [being] targeted .... There's no empathy, you know? It's 'Let's pick on the most "other" within the community'.... It's just sad because it's *actual lives*"—trans and gender nonconforming youths' lives.

In 2023, twenty anti-LGBTQ+ bills were proposed in the South Carolina legislature. In response, We Are Family co-led SC United for Justice and Equality, a coalition of more than twenty affirming organizations across the state and region, to speak out, testify, and advocate for equality. As the year came to a close, South Carolina was one of two southern states without a gender-affirming care ban (the other is Virginia). Despite heroic efforts from South Carolina advocates, including the We Are Family staff, a ban passed through the legislature in May 2024, becoming the twenty-fifth state with a law banning transgender youth from accessing this care.

•

As anti-trans bills pervade the South Carolina legislature—and as books are banned and GSAs challenged—Cora has seen hopelessness rise in the youth he works for and with. He says that youth are "trying to forge a path that cannot be seen."

"We had a conversation with one of our youth who's pursuing care. And she was like, 'Why are they doing this to me?'" Cora says. "'Did y'all tell these people that—that this is wrong? That this is hurting me?'"

Cora recounts the meeting they went to at the Statehouse in early 2024—to testify against the gender-affirming care ban. "It was 50 people there, and they all said, 'Please don't do this.' And they did it anyway." Only one person testified in favor of the bill during that subcommittee hearing.

She struggles with how to explain that to the youth she works with.

"What do you do with that type of hopelessness?" Cora asks. "And how do you tell them to go to the next meeting or submit another comment again?"

Even if they don't pass into law, the waves of anti-LGBTQ+ legislation being proposed across the US are having a tremendously negative impact on LGBTQ+ youth—especially their mental health. LGBTQ+ youth already experience stark disparities in terms of depression, suicidality, and anxiety, largely because of discrimination and lack of acceptance by family, friends, and society at large. The current political climate has only worsened mental health outcomes for this already vulnerable and marginalized population.

As discussed in chapter five, according to the Trevor Project's 2023 US National Survey on the Mental Health of LGBTQ Young People, 41 percent of LGBTQ+ young people seriously considered attempting suicide in the past year—and rates were higher for those who were trans, nonbinary, and/or BIPOC; 56 percent said they wanted mental healthcare in the past year and were unable to receive it; nearly 33 percent said their mental health was poor most or all of the time due to anti-LGBTQ+ policies and legislation; and 66 percent reported that hearing about potential state or local laws banning people from discussing LGBTQ+ people at school made their mental health worse.[2]

Because of this, We Are Family has been putting a lot of resources toward youth mental health. In addition to the Mental Health Assistance Program it launched in 2021, We Are Family also facilitates multiple social support groups for youth and young adults—and one for parents and caregivers of LGBTQ+ youth as well. "We are a lifeline for a lot of our clients, a lot of our youth," Jonatan says.

But Domenico makes it clear that the support they provide to youth is not a one-way street. Like Jonatan, working with youth at We Are Family helped them to become more comfortable with who they are as well. "Encouraging them to be their authentic selves and live their authentic lives, they pushed me to do that, too," Domenico says. During their two and a half years at We Are Family, Domenico came out as gender nonconforming and as part of the asexual community: "That is something that the youth have given me, so I'm really appreciative of that."

According to Domenico, there's a long, difficult road ahead in South Carolina, and even if all the LGBTQ+ organizations in the state combined, the need for services like We Are Family's would still be greater than what that "mega organization" could provide. Still, Domenico believes that the tide is shifting. "There's a long legacy of activism within this community, from Stonewall to now," he says. "Given all of those years and decades, there are so many people who get it versus who don't get it. There are so many more families in South Carolina and the South who have moved beyond the stereotype of, 'Oh, that's the queer uncle we never really talk about' to actually having conversations around the kitchen table. There are so many more folks who get it on the ground, who have empathy, whose hearts and minds have been touched by [LGBTQ+] issues."

A few years ago, We Are Family moved to a bigger office and opened its thrift store full-time. Along with the executive director at the time, Jonatan and Cora made curtains, put up decorations, and did all the nitty-gritty that grassroots work requires. Once, Cora stood on Jonatan's shoulders in platform boots to hang a disco ball from the thrift store's ceiling. "We're real grassroots," she and Jonatan used to joke, "Like, in the dirt."

Despite the hard work, Jonatan says it hasn't been difficult to dedicate himself to the cause. "A lot of our youth don't feel comfortable being themselves in public," he explains. "But this is where we step in as adults and say, 'Well, let me be that person. Let me make people uncomfortable so you can feel comfortable in the future. Let me be myself. And let me pave the way for you so when you become an adult and you graduate high school, you can feel safe in the street.'"

In the meantime, Jonatan, Domenico, Cora, and the whole

We Are Family team will keep working to create spaces for southern trans and queer youth so that they can grow up to be the "baddies" they're meant to be, as Jonatan says. "We really focus on celebrating queer joy . . . I don't call myself an activist. I'm just doing the work to celebrate our lives," he says. "A lot of us will be out there protesting, will be testifying. But when it comes to it, we are here for our youth more than ever." And no matter what lies ahead, Jonatan will keep being the kind of resource he needed when he was their age. "I want to know how we can plant the seeds to help them bloom."

Chapter Nine

The small, mostly brick building in Little Rock, Arkansas, that inTRANSitive calls home has had many lives. It used to be a hair salon, and the rooms were filled with the sounds of snipping scissors, folks laughing, and perhaps gossiping townspeople. Before that it was an auto shop, the main noises being the grinding of tools and the revving of engines.

Today, the space has been transformed into a community center for trans and gender nonconforming Arkansans. There is still plenty of laughter here—and, perhaps, gossip (but no revving engines)—yet there are also trans flags on the walls and signs that say things like, "Transphobia is a sin. Trans people are divine!" There's a community closet, where trans folks can get free gender-affirming clothing, as well as a food pantry. Onsite and online, inTRANSitive's diverse and multilingual staff provide health insurance enrollment assistance, harm reduction, mutual aid, and HIV-specific support, among other services.

During our Zoom interview, things seem rather hectic on their end. Tien, inTRANSitive's Policy Coordinator, tells us that some people have gathered at their community center to make art for a pro-Palestinian action later that day. Soon, two other staff members log on—Max, the organization's Northwest Arkansas Coordinator, who uses he/they pronouns and is "queer AF," and Jo'jo, a Black woman of trans experience who is inTRANSitive's Outreach Coordinator.

Max shares inTRANSitive's origin story. The organization was founded in 2017 by Rúmba Yambú and Brody Parrish Craig, Max's husband. The two were living in Northwest Arkansas—a region that's "pretty white"—and working at a transgender-serving nonprofit. There, Rúmba faced both microaggressions and "straight-up aggressions" because of their race and ethnicity. "They both left that organization and decided that they were going to make their own . . . based on racial justice and the experiences of trans migrants of color in Arkansas," Max shares. "In Northwest Arkansas, there were a couple of queer organizations . . . [but there] weren't necessarily spaces that were safe for everyone," including "folks of color" and "disabled folks."

From a conversation between two friends, inTRANSitive was born in a coffee shop in Northwest Arkansas—with a mission to create a truly inclusive space and to work for social justice that centered BIPOC and immigrant trans people, as well as others marginalized by mainstream LGBTQ+ organizations.

InTRANSitive's efforts quickly snowballed—from writing letters to trans and queer people in prisons, to encouraging a local goddess festival to change its trans-exclusionary policies, to hosting the region's first Trans Day of Visibility parade.

In 2019, the organization moved to Little Rock, though it still works across the state. At the time, inTRANSitive was operating on a $5,000 annual budget. They were scrappy, to say the least, but when they saw a need in their community—from mutual aid during the COVID-19 pandemic to a food pantry—they tried to fill it.

And then came the flood of legislative bills, which Tien rattles off: bathroom bills in 2017 and a medical ethics bill in 2019. However, by 2021, "the anti-trans legislation here [became] just unbelievable." In response, Rúmba and Tien mobilized volunteers and community members in an on-the-ground campaign to beat back eight anti-trans bills during the 2021 legislative session, showing up at the capitol almost every day and coordinating BIPOC, trans-led rallies. (Infamously, the Arkansas legislature passed the country's first gender-affirming care ban for minors that year.[1]) At the same time, Rúmba was actively mobilizing people online, reaching supporters as far away as Mexico and Australia with the stories of transgender people in Arkansas. Suddenly, inTRANSitive was in the national spotlight.

As donations came pouring in, inTRANSitive had to figure out what to do next. "We decided that we needed a space that nobody could take away from us," Tien says.

Jack, who uses any pronouns, was working at a grocery store in Arkansas at the time. They took leave from work to visit family in Mexico, and when they returned, they were told that they didn't have a job. Jack's then-partner had some friends who needed help remodeling a space. "I was like, 'That's cool, I've always wanted to do that kind of work,'" Jack says. "I show up and meet Rúmba and Tien. And they're showing me what they need done, and I'm like, 'All right, but I have no experience.'"

"Neither do we," they responded.

Jack laughs. "I'm like, 'Oh my god!' So we start fixing up the center." He was surprised to learn that the center was going to be for trans people. "I knew that I wasn't cis, but I didn't have the term for it, so once I started talking to them and hanging around, I learned about myself." Jack identified as nonbinary at first, but now describes himself as "agender."

Once the remodeling was done, Rúmba and Tien offered Jack a job; today, he's inTRANSitive's Community Care Coordinator.

"It was really nice to have something tangible after that terrible legislative session," Tien says. "To go from fighting at the capitol to painting new walls, ripping up floors, and creating this beautiful space."

•

Silas Hoffer (Grand Ronde, Yakama) also understands the importance of creating safe spaces for his community.

He is the Two-Spirit Programming Advocate for the Native American Youth and Family Center (NAYA) in Portland, Oregon, and uses they/he pronouns. Growing up in a rural area, Silas was unaware that Two-Spirit people existed—and didn't fully accept their own identity (as trans, nonbinary, and same-gender loving) until they were in their mid-twenties. "I grew up on and off the reservation," Silas shares. "I've always lived in really small areas, small towns . . . I call myself a 'country rez kid.'"

Silas didn't know anything about trans people until he was fourteen, when he saw a TV show with a transgender character: "I was like, 'Whoa, you can actually *do* that?'" He quickly became obsessed: "I kept talking about it with my mom. She was like, 'Do you think you're trans?'" The way Silas's mom said it made Silas realize that she didn't think being trans was a good thing. "I was like, 'No, I don't know, I'm not trans. Not me,'" he says. After that, they tried hard to fit in as a girl. "I went from being this huge tomboy to being super girly . . . but I didn't understand at the time why that didn't work for me."

Silas started his post-secondary career at a community college and transferred to the University of Oregon when he was twenty-one. "They taught my language there, which is the Yakama Sahaptin language," Silas says. "And when I learned that the language didn't have gendered pronouns, I was like, 'Oh, I'm gonna use "they" pronouns 'cause it's traditional.'"

Silas also chopped off their hair and "started dressing like a dude." "But I still didn't come out," they say. "I was still like, 'Maybe I'm just more butch.'"

After graduating in 2018, Silas decided that they wanted to work in Native communities. He saw listings for jobs on reservations but wasn't sure he would be fully accepted there. "I'm definitely queer presenting," he says, and at community events, "I have all these Native people surrounding me, and I should feel comfortable, but as soon as I come in the room, it's like they start staring at me."

Eventually, Silas saw an opening for a youth advocate at NAYA. After they got the job—and then took a group of trans youth to the Montana Two-Spirit Gathering—everything finally clicked for them. The Montana Two-Spirit Gathering is a multiday event made by and for Native, First Nations, and Indigenous Two-Spirit individuals and their partners, families, and friends.[2] Held in western Montana, the Gathering has been running for more than twenty-five years and includes traditional ceremonies, workshops and presentations, a pageant, opportunities for social connection, and a powwow on the final night.

Two-Spirit is an umbrella term for Native people who possess both male and female spirits and can encompass an Indigenous person's gender identity, sexual orientation, or both.[3] Historically, in most tribes, Two-Spirit individuals were considered neither men nor women and often held a distinct, alternative gender status with specialized work and religious roles.[4] "Oftentimes, we don't get to see our Two-Spirit ancestors," Silas explains. "What we're shown is Geronimo, Standing Bear, those types of figures. They're always men—which is great, [and] I love the men in our community—but it's never women, never Two-Spirit people."

At the Montana Gathering, Silas saw "a world where I could be accepted. Even though it was far away, and the Gathering only happens once a year, at least now I could connect with those people." A couple of months later, Silas came out as trans and began medically transitioning.

In 2021, Silas returned to the Montana Two-Spirit Gathering, where he was named Mr. Montana Two-Spirit—one of the royal titles awarded at the Gathering's pageant. He hadn't intended to run in the pageant, but an auntie convinced him. ("I was like, 'I can't really say no to an elder,'" he quips.) After his victory, Silas was profiled in a newspaper, where he talked about the long history of Two-Spirit people.[5] Overall, Silas used their win in the pageant to show "my community . . . that I exist—that we exist," they say. "We're out here, we're doing this work, and we're proud of who we are."

Silas has become a kind of Two-Spirit ambassador, sharing their histories at Tribal events throughout the country. He is usually well received, but occasionally does encounter some resistance. At one powwow, for example, he was standing up with royalty from other pageants and wearing a pride flag on his ribbon skirt (which he'd made himself). Then it was his turn to speak. "Everyone before and after [me]—the mic was working just fine. . . . As soon as I got to the mic, it started cutting out . . . I just waited until the mic came back on, and then I just kept speaking," Silas says. "I didn't get everything out that I wanted to say. But I didn't let that deter me either."

Silas adds that there were some "older ladies" who were glaring at them and other people who were "not cool with me being there." At the same time, many people came up to them and were "super excited" they were there—and that they were representing Two-Spirit people: "There was a youth who came up to me who said, 'I'm trans, and my family is having a hard time with it, and they're not really accepting.'"

Silas often meets trans youth—and adults—who are struggling to find acceptance in their homes and communities. "Every time I go to a new place, people come up to me [and] are happy I am there and wanna take a picture with me or tell me their story and want to connect," he says. "So it is really impactful . . . just knowing that there's so many of us out there who need this."

"One of the hardest things about being trans in this country, in this world, is feeling like you're in a place where you're always being stared at or you're always being thought about in some kind of exclusionary way from other people who don't understand you," says Morgan Wallace (Chickasaw), who was crowned Mr. Montana Two-Spirit in 2023. In spaces like the Montana Two-Spirit Gathering, Morgan says that Two-Spirit people like her can "forget that there is a world that does not care for me."

Morgan grew up in Oklahoma but moved to California when she was nineteen. She describes high school in Oklahoma as "horrendous, violent, un-inclusive" and awash in religion.

Today, Morgan is an active member of Bay Area American Indian Two-Spirits (BAAITS). Founded in 1999, BAAITS creates community and support for Two-Spirit, Indigiqueer, and LGBTQ+ relatives and allies, including through an annual powwow, which drew about 5,000 people in 2024.[6,7]

"I would also like to see people stop focusing on trans people so much and focus on actual problems," Morgan says of anti-trans legislators. "There are people dying, and you're worried if I take a shot every week or not. You're worried about what clothes I wear. You're worried about how I wear my hair . . . I'd like [lawmakers] . . . to be focused on something like anti-inflation bills and things to help people fucking live."

Morgan is a transfeminine Two-Spirit person who's "mostly woman identified." However, she noticed that Miss Montana Two-Spirit always went to someone who was a drag queen, while Mr. Montana Two-Spirit was awarded to a transmasculine person. "I felt that it was important to push that boundary," she explains.

In order to do so, she competed for Mr. Montana. In a

2023 article, Morgan told ICT News that, "I have masculinity in me. It's part of the Two-Spirit and it's something I hide from because the colonial world tells me I have to, and I saw this as an opportunity to embrace that in a way that doesn't adhere to colonial standards . . . I could be Mr. Montana and still be a woman. That's what being Two-Spirited is all about."[8]

Silas expands on this point, explaining how colonization—in addition to the forcible spread of Christianity among Indigenous peoples and Eurocentric white supremacy—is the reason why so many Tribal communities have lost their own cultural values around Two-Spirit people. He also says that there is a difference in cultural attitudes about Two-Spirit people between younger and older generations: "A lot of times it's the elders who are really resistant . . . to that inclusivity, and it's because they're from the boarding school era."

From the early 1800s to the mid-1900s, hundreds of thousands of Indigenous children were forcibly removed from their homes by the US government and sent to residential schools, where they were forced to "assimilate" to white, Eurocentric cultural norms. This included erasing Native customs and languages, requiring conversion to Christianity, and compelling students to comply with European values, including a strict gender binary. Along with cultural violence, children attending these schools suffered a range of abuses, including "rampant physical, sexual, and emotional abuse; disease; malnourishment; overcrowding; and lack of healthcare."[9] The schools were also responsible for the deaths of hundreds of Native children.[10] "Christianity was really hammered into them," Silas says. "And now a lot of Christianity is . . . really showing up in our own culture, our own cultural values, and we're not even realizing that that's where it comes from."

As Silas works to educate and support Indigenous communities to help them re-learn their histories, he wants to move beyond decolonizing—and toward "re-Indigenizing": "When I say decolonize, I mean we need to unlearn the things that have been forced onto us. And when I say re-Indigenize, that means we need to take those teachings that were from our culture, bring them back, and start thinking about how that fits into us as modern Native people." They add that, "We need to make the whole culture around us Indigenous and take out everything that's not meant for us and that was forced onto us. This includes reclaiming our healthy sexuality and desires, our Two-Spirit coming-of-age ceremonies, and our expansive gender diversity."

Today, at the age of thirty-one, Silas is creating safe spaces for Indigenous youth to gather at NAYA. Among these are the Two-Spirit Safe Space Alliance, an after-school group, and a Queer Prom, which in 2023 hosted more than 300 students from across the Portland Public School system and nearby reservations. "It's hard to find Two-Spirit community. We kind of have to look for each other and then make our own spaces," Silas shares. "It's important to have these spaces so that people can understand that . . . there are people out there who want them around and want them alive—want them to be themselves and will accept them as who they are."

Of course, the work Silas engages in comes with its share of difficulties, as the youth he deals with face multiple challenges—including bullying, discrimination, and familial rejection. "[Parents] think that by keeping [kids] away from understanding themselves as trans or queer that they're helping them or protecting them or something like that, but it's just the opposite. They only learn to hate themselves," Silas explains. "I suffered from suicidality for many years because I wasn't supported in being who I am. My mom kept me isolated. . . . At one point, she cut up my clothes—my tomboy clothes—and made me dress in girls' clothes, which was very traumatizing for me."

When Silas hears about the struggles that many trans youth have with their parents and guardians, they understand that "all I can do is really listen to them and validate their feelings . . . I can't really tell them, 'These are what options you have,' because they really don't have any, unless they wanna run away and be houseless." However, he is still able to offer them some hope. "'If you need support in these areas,'" he will tell them, "'we will find something that helps you.' So I guess I try and give a lot of that power back to them. I just try to show them as many options as I know that they *do* have."

In the meantime, Silas says that they will continue being "as authentic to myself as I can be so that I can show youth that it's okay—you can see me as an adult who's thriving, who's doing my best in the world."

•

In Arkansas, inTRANSitive has been met with its fair share of discrimination and harassment. Last year, their building was repeatedly vandalized. Rúmba has been harassed. Local police also gave the organization a hard time for letting kids from a nearby school drop in for snacks and to do homework. "The whole thing with the laws being introduced about trans people being predators, we didn't want to take a risk," Jack explains. "So we unfortunately had to stop allowing them to come in." (Though this didn't stop them from doing LGBTQ+ youth-specific programs.) Mostly, though, she says the local community leaves them alone—aside from someone who, every so often, comes in looking for a hair stylist or a mechanic. "We're like, 'My guy, we don't have these parts,'" she jokes.

As is true in many red states across the country, the larger environment in which inTRANSitive operates is inhospitable. "The overall climate of Arkansas is fucking scary," Tien says. However, according to Tien, the greatest problem many transgender youth face is not gender-affirming care bills, but poverty. "A lot of kids in Arkansas don't even have the privilege of being worried about the legislative effects" of bad bills, Tien explains. "Our state has a lot of poverty, and there is a lot of intentionality with politicians here to keep people poor and sick." Tien talks about food deserts, a housing crisis, and a far-right supermajority in the state government as just some of the many things that keep people in poverty.

For trans youth in Arkansas, Max chimes in, "knowing that . . . the place that you've been born and raised hates you and wants you to die or be invisible—that's a really, really hard thing to sit with."

"Everybody deserves to live and that's what our cause is—for us to live," Jo'jo adds. Her first exposure to the organization was at a transfemme event. "I remember meeting back when I was still homeless . . . in 2020," Jo'jo says. She immediately felt a lot of love from the staff and volunteers—they weren't judgmental, and they were standing up for something good. Now Jo'jo is one of inTRANSitive's newest staff members. "It's my first experience ever doing any type of work like this on the frontlines," she says. "It feels like we're just doing something that's right."

Mike is inTRANSitive's Immigrant Rights Organizer. A transgender immigrant from El Salvador, Mike says—through an interpreter—that economic challenges are what impact trans immigrants in Arkansas the most. It's hard to find an affordable place to live, he explains, and to find jobs that pay well enough. In addition to the usual hurdles they face, immigrants are also discriminated against if they're trans or queer.

Mike came to the United States with his family three years ago. Their economic situation was precarious, and the family didn't know any lawyers who could help them with the immigration process. Finally, someone told Mike that he should talk with Rúmba—who ended up helping him and his family access the legal support they needed to apply for asylum. Mike now helps other immigrants with migration matters and to access the socioeconomic support they need. "Many people think coming here, things will be different from Latin American countries," he says. "But there's nothing different."

He adds that many people believe that in the United States there is freedom of expression and that LGBTQ+ people's lives are not endangered. In El Salvador, Mike explains, most transgender people don't live to be thirty-five. In the United States, though, trans people's lives are still at risk. And the anti-trans laws being proposed are worse than those in many Latin American countries. Today, he says, it's like "it's a crime to be trans" in the US.

"I think there's hope that if we keep showing up, and we keep telling them, 'You can't stop us from existing,'—and the ACLU keeps suing people—we'll make progress," Max says. "It's just *really hard* to make and maintain progress. Because the deck is stacked so intensely against us."

To keep the fight for progress going, inTRANSitive works at every level it can—alongside other activists and advocates across the United States—getting resources to youth and under-resourced groups that other organizations have left behind or pushed out to the margins. The inTRANSitive staff protest. They host rallies. They build coalitions. They testify. They distribute food. They help survivors of intimate partner violence. They hand out hygiene kits, clothing, and condoms. They have workshops and trainings. "If folks need it," Tien states, "We got it—or we get it."

"Our efforts are not going unnoticed," Jo'jo says about the impact inTRANSitive is having on trans people's daily lives. For example, Jo'jo is currently working with a Black trans mother who has an adopted child: "She's homeless right now, but she's *this close* to moving into an apartment." Jo'jo knows how much stable housing can change things. "I was homeless for two years—I got through that," she says. Today, she has a job, a home, and a puppy named Uno.

Although the legislative landscape looks bleak, Max is hopeful about the future. He recalls attending Northwest Arkansas Pride in June 2023 and seeing so many "trans kids with trans flags and nonbinary flags and rainbow makeup and face paint and shit like that . . . I cried a lot." Of those youth, Max adds that, "They're gonna grow up and they're gonna change the world, just like I did, and the people before me, and the people before that. They're not gonna give up."

Chapter Ten

"I thought there was something wrong with me . . . I actually tried taking my life a couple of weeks before the first kin•dom camp. Fortunately, I'm still alive," a fifteen-year-old boy said in a 2024 interview.[1]

When the boy's mother suggested he go to kin•dom camp, a weeklong LGBTQ+ camp for youth ages twelve to seventeen in East Texas, he agreed—but not because he wanted to go to camp: "I viewed camp more as my chance to, you know, finally, like, take my life in a way that wouldn't impact my parents because they wouldn't have to find me."

But something changed when he arrived. People were warm and welcoming and met him "with open arms." "I had the opportunity to meet an adult—a trans man, actually, and his wife—who, I think to put it lightly, saved my life," the boy shares. "I'm seeing a straight trans man out here, dating a cis woman . . . with the woman actually just loving her husband as a man, as he is. [It] was a pivotal point for me. It was like, it's not impossible."

Reverend Dr. John Leedy, who identifies as bisexual, didn't come out until he was well into adulthood—though he knew something was different about himself from a young age. In high school, he learned the word bisexual, but he still closeted himself. Then, he went to a small, conservative college in West Texas that actually levied a daily fine against students who came out, "until you signed this document recanting being gay." "I couldn't afford to be gay," John says with a laugh.

As a Presbyterian minister, John felt like he had to choose between his calling and being himself—at the time he entered the ministry, the Presbyterian Church (USA) wasn't fully affirming toward LGBTQ+ people (and wouldn't be until 2011). "Just knowing that there are Christians out there—there are people of faith out there—that believe" in an affirming and inclusive theology, "would have been enough for me," John says. "To be able to go through high school thinking that there's not something broken and sinful and wrong and dirty and shameful about this thing that I didn't ask to be—that just *is*, you know?"

In 2022 and 2023, John was a counselor at kin•dom camp. His favorite moment was when the young people first arrived: "They open the door, and here's this cabin common room covered in rainbows, and they see their flag up on the wall. And here's their camp counselor with a big old [bisexual] lanyard around his neck saying, 'Welcome to your cabin . . . pick a bunk.'"

Unlike many youth camps, the cabins aren't gender segregated at kin•dom camp. Gender-neutral restrooms are abundant. And most of the staff are LGBTQ+. "I love to watch their faces when they realize that they don't have to do the math of 'who do I need to be in this space,'" John says. "They can put that down and realize that they can just be themselves here in this radical way that doesn't exist outside of spaces like this."

Now the Executive Director of kin•dom camp, John's face lights up as he describes what the camp is like for the LGBTQ+ youth they serve. There are affirming counselors, nurses, licensed professional counselors, and behavioral health specialists—as well as a two-to-one ratio of campers to adult staff. Each day, the campers fill out adhesive nametags; if they decide to change their names or pronouns, the staff use the new ones. "It gives trans and nonbinary young people the ability to try on different names, different pronouns—see what fits, what works," John shares. The camp also holds space for neurodivergent campers and those with chronic illnesses and disabilities (so they aren't "squirreled away in a corner" but are given the supports they need to participate in "every part of camp"). Campers also meet LGBTQ+ adults who show them that it's possible to thrive as a queer and trans person.

Kin•dom camp offers LGBTQ+ youth the same activities as many other summer camps—canoeing, kayaking, ziplining, archery, arts and crafts—but in a space "where your truest self gets to find its way into the world," John says.

The camp was the brainchild of Andy Hackett, a young trans man from Texas. As a child, Andy had gone to regular youth camps and enjoyed them. Later, when he became a staff member at a camp for young people with celiac disease (hosted at a faith-based camp and conference site), Andy wondered aloud to Reverend Pepa Paniagua (a queer Presbyterian minister) and camp counselor Garrett deGraffenreid about how awesome it would be to have a camp for LGBTQ+ teenagers.

Pepa, Andy, Garrett, and Baylee Davis became the initial leadership team at kin•dom camp. They hosted the first week-long camp session for almost sixty young people in the summer of 2022 in East Texas.[2] In 2023, the organization ran two camps—adding a second one at Zephyr Point in Lake Tahoe, Utah. In 2024, they plan to facilitate camps in four states—Texas, Utah, Illinois, and Indiana.

John explains that the founders of kin•dom camp chose the word "kindom" instead of "kingdom" because it comes from "mujarista, Latina theology" which offers an alternative worldview to traditional systems of power and empire—including the Christian idea of the "kingdom of God." "Kingdom became synonymous with power over—instead of solidarity with," John explains. "Kindom was this idea that the way that we interact with God and with one another is as kin, as siblings, as friends." He goes on to say that kindom "re-equalizes" power so that it's something "shared communally instead of hierarchically."

"Instead of the church saying, 'Okay, who deserves a place at the table?'" John says, "it's the church saying 'We don't own this table anymore.'"

While affirming Christian themes were initially central to kin•dom camp's programming, since so many LGBTQ+ youth have experienced religious trauma from faith-based institutions, the camp's leadership has shifted away from centering faith and religion, instead focusing on queer and trans identities—including history, culture, joy, mental health, and other topics. As a result, they now host youth from different faith backgrounds—including Jewish, Christian, and New Age—as well as those who are atheist. "Our goal is to welcome, affirm, and celebrate *everything* these young people bring in," John shares.

•

Almost 1,000 miles away from East Texas, in Columbia, South Carolina, a diverse group of young people are gathered for a warm meal on a cool spring evening in the fellowship hall of a church. A member of the church, Michael Watson, stands in front of the group to welcome them. He tells them this is an LGBTQ+-affirming space for youth ages fourteen to twenty-three, and he asks that everyone here treat each other with respect.

Some of the young people present already know Michael, as he's visited them at the transitional youth shelters that dot Columbia's cityscape. Others have heard about Safe Space Dinners through a friend. Not everyone here is LGBTQ+, but most are. (This makes sense, given that LGBTQ+ youth represent an estimated 40 percent of the youth houseless population, and 28 percent experience housing insecurity during their lives.[3,4]) Often, there's entertainment—from improv performers from a local community theater to karaoke to DJs. There's always a hair stylist and mental health professionals on hand, as well as other services, like HIV testing and safer sex kits.

When Michael talks to people in Columbia about Safe Space Dinners, their first reaction is usually surprise. "People will go, 'This is in South Carolina?'" he says with a laugh. But *he's* usually surprised by what comes next. "The next thing that's said is not anything derogatory about it. It's like, 'Wow, how can I help?'"

Michael originally proposed the idea for Safe Space Dinners to the South Carolina Synod for the Evangelical Lutheran Church in America (ELCA) in 2019. Along with other volunteers from Reformation Lutheran Church—one of only six affirming ELCA congregations in the state[5]—and with grant funding from the synod, Michael planned to put on the first dinner in August 2020. Then, the pandemic happened. The timeline shifted, and after more than a year of planning, the first dinner was held in August 2021.

But no one came.

For the following month's dinner, they put ads inside buses and distributed stickers with QR codes.

Again, no one came.

"We went for quite some time without having anyone attend," Michael recalls. He realized they couldn't keep asking folks to volunteer to cook dinners and have nobody show up to eat them. The planning team did some research, as well as deep soul-searching, and saw their missteps. "What we were lacking was not just reach but credibility," he says. Michael and his team of volunteers then began reaching out to organizations already serving youth facing housing insecurity. They started getting to know the staff at these agencies—as well as the youth themselves. They went to shelters and housing programs. They built trust. And they proved they weren't trying to convert anyone—or send them to conversion therapy. "Every church says all are welcome. . . . They're gonna get you in the door. And then come the caveats," Michael says, "'Yeah, you're welcome—as long as you will let us start to change you. And we're changing you in the name of God.'"

Michael wanted to make sure that the LGBTQ+ youth who came to Safe Space Dinners knew that they were truly welcome—as their full, authentic selves. At the same time, on advice from Parity, a similar program in New York City, Michael and his group expanded their population from *only* LGBTQ+ youth to any youth who were houseless or housing insecure.

"They said, 'You've got to realize that while you're wanting to serve these LGBTQ youth who are homeless or housing insecure, they have formed friendships on the streets with people who aren't necessarily LGBTQ, and if you ask them to come without their friends, they're not gonna come,'" Michael says. "So, we focused on making a very deliberate choice to be a very affirming space."

After that, word spread, and soon, dozens of youth were showing up to the monthly dinners in Reformation Lutheran Church's fellowship hall. In 2023, attendance averaged twenty to forty youth per meal, and by early 2024, the program boasted forty community partners, a slew of volunteers, two Master of Social Work interns from the nearby University of South Carolina, and a partner church—St. Martin's-in-the-Fields Episcopal Church—that has started hosting a second monthly dinner.

Michael, who attends Reformation Lutheran Church with his husband, Bryan, says that youth houselessness has been at the forefront of his mind for a long time. He used to donate to national organizations addressing the crisis among LGBTQ+ youth, like True Colors United.[6] But then he was nudged into this project by a friend at church and put together a grant proposal with his husband's support.

Michael shares a story about a couple who came to one of their dinners. Both were genderfluid youth and had been kicked out of their houses because of their relationship. "That's not an uncommon story," Michael explains. The two had nothing but an "old broken-down car," which they lived in. At Safe Space Dinners, "they found a place to get a good hot meal, a place to get a bag of supplies and entertainment—and somewhere that really expresses to them that they're appreciated for who they are." Michael says that the couple comes to Safe Space Dinners almost every month and have now moved up what he calls "the housing ladder"—finding stable housing in town.

Michael says that the dinners connect youth to a host of resources, but more than anything, they provide an affirming human connection. "I think that makes a very important difference—especially in a place like South Carolina," he says. "Without those connections, you know how badly those situations can go."

•

Reverend Debra Hopkins has experienced houselessness herself—which is one of the reasons she launched her own transitional housing program for transgender folks in Charlotte, North Carolina.

Debra came out as trans while pastoring at a Baptist church in Dacula, Georgia, in the late 1980s and early 1990s—which also happened to be her first pastoral position. Before coming out, she says that "Preachers like myself were casting LGBTQ+ people out." As she transitioned, Debra's mind—and theology—transformed as well. "If we say that God is love and all are welcome," she states, "I don't see any footnotes or anything that says, 'Well, except for this particular body of people, or this community.'"

Debra dug deep into scripture and began to understand it through a different lens. Over time, she grew to have a theology that could "bridge all of God's children, even those who were being ostracized and cast from their faith . . . because they wanted to live as their true, authentic selves."

From there, Debra's ministry took her across the South—where she often supported efforts in her churches to help those who were houseless or suffering from violence or other inequities. After experiencing multiple traumas at the hands of law enforcement and the legal system in Alabama in the late 2000s, Debra moved to Charlotte to get a fresh start. But health problems, including the temporary loss of her eyesight due to diabetic retinopathy,[7] got in her way. Eventually, she found herself sleeping in parks. On occasion, she was kicked out of women's shelters for being trans.

Transgender people like Debra—and especially those who are BIPOC—are deeply impacted by housing insecurity. According to the 2017 US Transgender Survey, over their lifetimes, 30 percent of transgender people in the United States—and 51 percent of Black trans women like Debra—experience houselessness.[8] This rate is even higher (75 percent) for trans people whose immediate family have thrown them out of their homes. Among transgender Americans who have stayed in shelters, the majority (70 percent) have encountered at least one negative experience, such as being forced out, harassed, or attacked.[9]

For two and a half years, Debra was houseless. Finally, someone saw her enter a park one night and called the police. But instead of arresting her, the police connected Debra with mental health services and healthcare. With the help of the team at Monarch, a North Carolina agency that provides health and supportive services, Debra got her blood sugar levels into a healthy range, regained her eyesight, and entered Monarch's transitional housing program.

Back on her feet, Debra was determined to give back to her community. In 2015, she launched the first transitional housing program for transgender folks in Charlotte, called There's Still Hope. She says that she wants the trans community to realize that "you do belong and that you have purpose."

Debra has recently stepped away from the frontlines. In early 2024, she moved to South Carolina, where she now owns her own home. While There's Still Hope's housing program has closed, Debra is in the process of transforming the organization into one that can provide training and technical assistance to nonprofits working with trans communities.

Debra dreams that one day, the LGBTQ+ community will come together to push for transgender-affirming transitional housing in every major city in North Carolina—and beyond.

But she notes, too often, the lesbian and gay communities "table the T."

•

In Williamsburg, Virginia, Rabbi David Katz helms Temple Beth El, a sixty-four-year-old welcoming congregation. "One of the adjectives that is often used to describe our congregation is *haimish*[10]—it's very warm and welcoming," Rabbi David says. "Especially for our kids and our teenagers, my number one goal is that the synagogue feels like a place where they can be themselves, and where they can feel safe, and where they can feel at home."

Rabbi David describes Williamsburg as a "purple voting place" where there are not a lot of Jews and not a lot of diversity. "It's a tricky place to be Jewish. It's a tricky place to be gay or lesbian. It's a tricky place to be trans or genderfluid," he explains. Rabbi David wants Temple Beth El to be the solution to those issues. "For kids who don't necessarily fit into a neat and easy box, this can be a place where those kids can struggle, and the synagogue is there for them—there's no judgment, there's no questioning, there's no criticism. . . . And they therefore learn that that's what Judaism is," he says proudly. He pauses, then adds: "That's not the case in a lot of other places."

Along with leading a local synagogue, Rabbi David founded

and co-runs a multifaith organization called Historic Area Religions Together, or HART (also an LGBTQ+-affirming group). The month before we spoke, the group had sponsored an Iftar dinner at a local church, breaking bread with friends across faith communities in honor of the holy month of Ramadan.

"There were eighty people in a room," Rabbi David recounts. "There were Muslims, there were Jews, there were Christians, there were Quakers, there were Unitarians, and everybody came together to listen to Turkish Muslims chant prayers about Ramadan and to share a meal with each other." Rabbi David believes that this kind of interfaith communication is essential to bringing people together: "Every time I see people talking to each other who come from different places and different backgrounds, who are bringing together communities of difference . . . that gives me hope."

Austen Petersen joins our Zoom interview donning a pink and white baseball shirt that boldly proclaims, "Protect Trans Youth." The Director of Religious Education at the Williamsburg Unitarian Universalist (WUU) congregation, Austen explains that WUU has been a Welcoming Congregation for the past twenty-five years and that that inclusivity is informed by the "work that we've been doing for the past 200 years." "Unitarian Universalists were the first to ordain a woman, and then they just kept going," Austen says.

It was the inspiring example of a trans person that made

Austen decide to become a Unitarian Universalist (UU) in the first place. In the late 2000s, at a peace rally in Akron, Ohio, Austen saw Susan Davis, a trans woman from a local UU congregation, speaking to a large crowd. She talked about being a Green Beret and "how nobody desires peace more than a service member." She also shared information about her transition. The "sheer grit" and "embodied love" that Susan showed that day was "astonishing" to Austen.

During her speech, Susan mentioned attending the Unitarian Universalist Church of Akron. "I went to the UUCA website, and lo and behold, they were hiring a religious education assistant," Austen recalls. Now, more than fifteen years later, Austen continues to serve the UU—and help LGBTQ+ communities. One of the programs that WUU is engaged in to support LGBTQ+ youth (and adults) is Our Whole Lives, an age-appropriate, science-based, inclusive sexuality education curriculum that is broken into age groups that run from kindergarten and first graders to older adults. "We have a Welcoming Congregation team that meets regularly, and they talk about all the attacks on trans bodies that are happening and what can we do to be helpful, both legislatively and also spiritually," Austen explains. WUU also hosts Pride events, Trans Day of Remembrance services, and other workshops. In addition, they participate in Advocacy Days at the state capitol, where people of faith and ordained ministers gather to say "I am a person of faith, and I absolutely believe that trans people are divine. Don't you dare do anything to make them feel otherwise."

Working with LGBTQ+ youth every day, Austen worries about their health, mental health, and rights. Austen is frustrated that we're asking young people "to be the adults in the room"—to speak up for themselves at school board meetings and go toe-to-toe with school administrators over bathroom rights. Austen says we keep asking kids to be agile and patient—to go totally online when COVID hit, to wait their turn for vaccines (which were released for adults first), and to keep "attending school board meetings and arguing with people who are perfectly comfortable spewing hateful rhetoric." "It just breaks my heart," Austen adds. "So much is being thrown at them—who wouldn't be anxious? Who wouldn't be depressed if put in that situation? If our basic needs are not being met or are under threat of not being met, that's not going to produce the best outcome. And so it's the adults' job to make sure that all kids are getting their basic needs met—so kids can just go be kids."

•

Liam Hooper entered divinity school when he was forty-nine years old—the same year he took his very first shot of testosterone.

Growing up in North Carolina, Liam attended a Baptist church with his family, but says that "the God thing gave me the willies—in terms of God's people." Liam's grandmother, however, had a very different version of God. She was of Scottish-Muskogee heritage, and Liam came to understand the spirituality she shared with him as a mix of Celtic and Indigenous practices. "She told me about God by teaching me about irises and making pies," he remembers. "This very personal—but yet shot-through-everything, present-everywhere-and-yet-nowhere—God you could find in geodes and irises and lilies and chickadees and hawks and fossils and history did not match what I saw in the church." His grandmother's idea of God helped Liam "tune out the people who called me an abomination. Who spit at me when I was growing up. Who threw gum in my hair. Who barked at me when I was going down the hallway. Who beat my ass—because I confused them."

His grandmother's sense of the divine eventually led Liam to divinity school. He went on to become an ordained minister in the United Church of Christ (UCC) but eventually resigned his standing in the UCC and converted to Judaism. Today, he and his spouse are members of a temple in Winston-Salem, North Carolina.

Liam's 2020 book, *Trans-Forming Proclamation: A Transgender Theology of Daring Existence*, "put[s] the lived experience of gender-transcendent peoples . . . at the center of a creative and constructive theological project."[11] Liam explains the idea behind a transgender theology: "There's a trans theology that is a way of doing theology. A way or a practice of encountering, reading, thinking about, being curious about, reflecting on, questioning, contending, arguing with, and identifying possible meanings—which usually leads to more questions and implications in and through the texts we call sacred."

Liam adds that, much like trans-ness, religion or spirituality are also about "being and becoming a person, seeking formational transformative experiences that paradoxically are essential to becoming more fully and consciously who it is in us to be and become. . . . It's this constant search for the ineffable in the physical." He pauses. "There's nothing much more trans than that."

Beyond these heady academic conversations, Liam is energized by seeing faith in action—especially in interfaith spaces. For several years, he was involved in interfaith advocacy and organizing efforts in the Winston-Salem area, beginning with North Carolina Amendment 1 in 2012, which defined marriage as being between a man and a woman,[12] and House Bill 2 (HB 2), the anti-trans bathroom bill from 2016.

Along with these efforts, Liam has joined clergy and lay leaders from various traditions in supporting each other's work toward community-building and seeking justice. "If something tragic happened, we would have these huge vigils," Liam shares. "It was so beautiful and so healing for so many of us because it wasn't just us as queer folks taking care of each other, it was people really trying to get in the deep work with us. To be allies . . . . To be spiritual friends."

He remembers cohosting a multifaith vigil at Parkway United Church of Christ after the Pulse shooting in 2016, when forty-nine people were killed at an LGBTQ+ nightclub in Orlando, Florida.[13] Liam had invited a local Muslim leader to attend who was not part of the LGBTQ+ community but had collaborated with Liam and the interfaith community on several justice initiatives. But Liam didn't know if the imam would attend because he had prayers to lead that night.

The vigil started. A few songs were sung, and the opening speakers shared their words of grief and compassion. When he was about to introduce the next speaker, Liam looked up and saw the imam at the back of the sanctuary. He invited him to sit with the other clergy at the front of the room and asked if he would like to speak. The imam nodded. Liam paraphrases the imam's speech: "So when you asked me to be here, I got my people started for prayers, and I came here because why wouldn't I be here? You have stood with me when you didn't have to, when it put you in harm's way. How could I not stand with you?"

When it comes to faith, Liam wishes that people would stop focusing on saving souls and pay more attention to saving lives. "Why do you worry about saving somebody's soul? If you did, you're not gonna know how that turned out anyway," he says, laughing. "I feel certain that how you don't love God is by making laws against people—restricting their movement . . . telling them what they can and cannot do with their own bodies in their own homes, how they can perceive or understand their own bodies, who they can love and who they cannot, which God is the right God." Instead, he suggests that faith communities should "give people interfaith and multifaith ways to come together [and] do things that build and create community. . . . Do things that aren't about standing in the pulpit and giving a sermon. Have pizza just for the sake of having pizza. Get together and sing."

Austen similarly believes that creating spaces of joy for LGBTQ+ kids is important, which is a focus at Williamsburg Unitarian Universalists. "If we can be part of the giggle process, that would really be ideal," Austen says, citing the youth and child game nights hosted by WUU. "It's just so important to have that outlet for social emotional intelligence and development, but also for a break. Like, all anybody here wants to do is play *Dungeons and Dragons*. 'Are you in? Are you a dragon? Let's go . . . . Depending on how things continue to go, part of resiliency both at the community level and also for the individual will be building and continuing to embrace moments of joy. Because that's what's gonna get us through."

•

Both Michael Watson and John Leedy hope that one day, their programs will no longer be needed.

"I'll miss the kids," Michael says, but he'd rather them be in safe, loving, and accepting families and homes.

John, too, says he hopes that "every camp, every week, every session will be a safe, affirming, and celebratory space for every kid that walks through the door. Or the tent flap."

In the current political climate, though, that seems like a tall order. John ticks off a few of the many challenges facing trans and queer youth today: "loss of access to healthcare, dissolving of GSAs at their public schools, and censorship in public libraries, where any kind of material that is aware of or affirming of queer experience of any kind is stripped off the shelves." Ultimately, "there's just this relentless debate over their personhood," he says. And "it's everywhere." For instance, John shares that the day kin•dom camp announced it was hosting a 2024 camp in Indiana, the State House of Representatives proposed legislation to "nullify gay marriage and to forbid it moving forward."

But news like that makes John even more determined to expand kin•dom camp to what he calls "the danger states." "We're looking at the places where a space like this is truly going to be a lifesaving and life-affirming place," he says.

Each summer, John sees just how life-affirming safe and brave spaces like kin•dom camp can be. For example, the Dress Code Project provides free haircuts for campers. Nervous, the kids settle themselves in a chair and tell the stylist what they'd like done. Clippers buzz and scissors snip, and as the campers sneak a glance in the mirror, they get—perhaps for the first time in their lives—a glimpse of themselves becoming who they are.

When they're done, the campers hop out of their chairs and walk through a glittery rainbow curtain that's strung across the door. It's like they're walking out on a runway, and as they emerge, campers and counselors clap and whistle and cheer. Nerves gone, the kids smile—the biggest, brightest smiles you've ever seen.

"Our job is to create the space," John shares, "and let that queer and trans joy and magic happen."

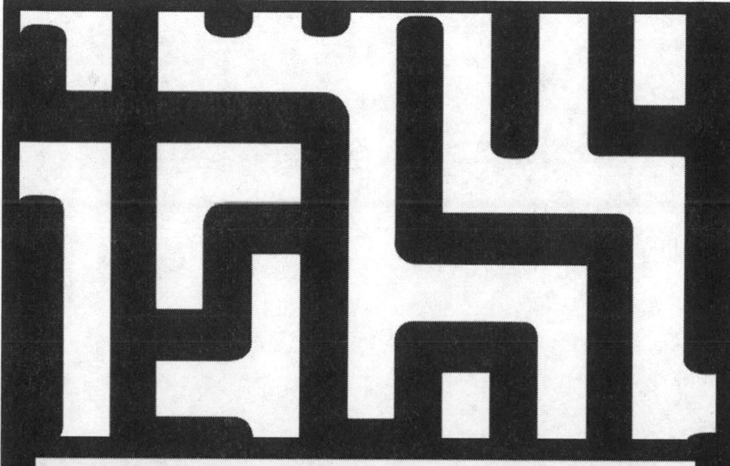

TAKE ACTION & TAKE CARE

Take Action & Take Care

TAKE ACTION

There are many ways to take action in support of transgender youth at this critical time. Here are just a few things you can do to make a difference in your community:

Be an Advocate

To get involved in advocacy efforts in your town or state, reach out to statewide and community LGBTQ+ organizations like the ones referenced in this book. There are many amazing groups to get tapped into for action, from Georgia Equality to Louisiana Trans Advocates to Freedom Oklahoma. There are also wonderful coalitions bringing groups to statehouses across the country to share their testimonies with lawmakers, organize rallies and protests for LGBTQ+ justice, and support legal efforts to overturn discriminatory laws. Find an organization near you that aligns with your values, and get involved in supporting the trans people in your life.

Start Small

As Satya says in chapter five, small acts of kindness and resistance add up. So, if you're not ready to head to the statehouse (or you've already done so and need a break), think of the small things you can do to become a firefly in the world. Perhaps you can show support to a trans or queer friend who's having a hard time. Or maybe you can support a trans BIPOC artist by buying or sharing their work. Support organizations that serve and advocate for trans and queer youth—like Safe Space Dinners or OUTMemphis.

Share Stories

We know that what truly changes hearts and minds are the stories we tell each other. The stories in this book represent a diversity of experiences—but they are only a handful of the stories of trans people and those who love them, and there are so many more to be told (including, perhaps, your own). Seek out stories from people who are like—or *not* like—you. Write/draw/sing your own story. And if and when you are safe or able to do so, share it with others. Finally, listen—especially to your friends and loved ones who are furthest out on the margins—and center their voices when you can.

Many of the people we spoke to in this book painted pictures of a potential future where trans youth are loved and fully affirmed as their amazing selves. Imagine what that world would look like—and don't give up hope that it can come to be.

Help us make that future a reality—one small step at a time.

TAKE CARE

One thing that nearly everyone we interviewed for this book highlighted was the importance of creating community. In today's climate, we need each other more than ever, so think about the ways in which you can connect. Find a support group where you can meet other LGBTQ+ youth or families. Share a meal with your neighbors or go to a Trans Day of Visibility event. If you're a person of faith, stop by an affirming faith or interfaith community and see how you can get involved. Whether you meet folks online or in person, know that you don't have to go it alone.

For Parents/Caregivers/Family Members/Allies

If you or your family are impacted by anti-trans bills, either directly or indirectly, finding community is critical. Always remember that there are people across the country who are on the same journey as you. Some great places to start finding support groups and other resources (either virtual or in person) are PFLAG (pflag.org) and TransParent (transparentusa.org).

If your child needs gender-affirming care and you live in a state where that is not legal, please reach out to the Trans Youth Emergency Project (TYEP) for help (southernequality.org/tyep). When you live in a state where gender-affirming care is banned, it can feel like there are no options—but TYEP can serve as a bridge to make sure your child gets the care they need.

For parents, caregivers, or family members who want to be better allies to trans youth, listen to them and their stories. Believe them when they tell you who they are—and seek ways to support them. But don't forget—trans kids are still kids. Their transness isn't their only defining trait. Be a part of the "giggle process," as Austen Petersen calls it—if they love to read books or shoot hoops or play *Dungeons and Dragons*, ask them about the books they like, grab a basketball, or ask them what they think of gelatinous cubes. None of us are one-note humans—and neither are trans kids.

For Young Trans Folks

If you are a young trans person, remember that there are many people out there who are fighting for you. Tap into LGBTQ+ youth organizations, affirming groups, and community centers to experience the abundance of love that is pouring in your direction. Maybe there is an organization like We Are Family (waf.org) in your town that is throwing a queer prom. Some other great examples of community centers include OUTMemphis (www.outmemphis.org) in Tennessee, inTRANSitive (www.intransitive.org) in Arkansas, the Glo Center (www.glocenter.org) in Missouri, and Kaleidoscope Youth Center (www.kycohio.org) in Ohio—among many others. CenterLink offers a directory of LGBTQ+ centers online at www.lgbtqcenters.org.

If it's hard to find LGBTQ+ groups for youth in your community or school, look for virtual support. Some state and regional LGBTQ+ organizations offer online programming for youth. At a national level, The Trevor Project (www.thetrevorproject.org/visit-trevorspace) has more than 500 online clubs through its TrevorSpace program (for youth ages thirteen to twenty-four). Some PFLAG programs offer virtual meetings for youth and their families. And Queer Youth Assemble (www.queeryouthassemble.org) hosts in-person and virtual activities throughout the United States.

You can also join the GSA at your school—or if you don't have one, see if you can start one. You can get more resources on finding or starting GSA clubs at the GSA Network (www.gsanetwork.org). Even if you can't have a GSA at your school due to discriminatory policies, see if you can find or start one at a community center like NAYA, a library, or in other affirming community spaces.

If you are in need of gender-affirming care and you live in a state where that care is not legal, please reach out to the Trans Youth Emergency Project for help (southernequality.org/tyep).

For Trans Adults

While this book is aimed at transgender youth and their families, if you are a trans adult, we want you to know you are also not alone! We want to see trans youth become trans adults, and we want trans adults to feel safe, loved, affirmed—and protected. It can be so hard to watch the steady erosion of human rights in this country and feel fear about trans futures. But we hope the stories in this book remind you that there are others out there—both trans folks and allies—who are working hard to build communities, share resources, and fight for equity and justice. We welcome you to join (or continue) this fight.

At the same time, it is so important to sustain yourself—with community, with joy, and with care for yourself. So, use some of the resources outlined above to find community groups and access supportive services. Share your stories and make art. Join a trans-inclusive board game or *D and D* group and giggle as you fight off an owlbear. Find affirming affinity groups or faith communities. Consider joining a team hosted by a local chapter of Stonewall Sports (www.stonewallsports.org). Look for trans-friendly groups on Meetup. And if you can't find a group, consider creating one.

Finally, the Campaign for Southern Equality's *Trans in the South Guide* (www.transinthesouth.org) is a useful tool that can help you find the medical, legal, and other resources to continue living with autonomy and dignity.

WHAT NEXT?

To learn more about some of the amazing organizations featured and discussed in this book, please visit the websites below:

American Civil Liberties Union – https://aclu.org/
Bay Area American Indian Two-Spirits – https://www.baaits.org/
Campaign for Southern Equality – https://southernequality.org/
Elevated Access – https://www.elevatedaccess.org/
The GenderCool Project – https://gendercool.org/
GLSEN – https://www.glsen.org/
inTRANSitive – https://www.intransitive.org/
Kentucky Health Justice Network – https://www.kentuckyhealthjusticenetwork.org/
kin•dom camp – https://kindomcommunity.org/
Lambda Legal – https://lambdalegal.org/
NAYA Family Center – https://nayapdx.org/
OUTMemphis - https://www.outmemphis.org/
PFLAG National – https://pflag.org/
Queer Youth Assemble – https://queeryouthassemble.org/
QMed – https://queermed.com/
Safe Space Dinners – https://reformationcae.org/safe-space-dinners/
Temple Beth El – https://tbewilliamsburg.org/
The T.R.A.N.S. Program – https://www.transprogram.org/

Trans Social – https://transsocial.org/
The Trevor Project – https://www.thetrevorproject.org/
We Are Family – https://waf.org/
Williamsburg Unitarian Universalists – https://wuu.org/
Youth Action Fund – https://www.youthactionfund.org/

The list of organizations that are meeting this moment is changing as rapidly as the legal landscape for trans youth. To keep up with this ever-shifting environment, CSE has built an online resource center where you can find more information about organizations doing important work across the US for LGBTQ+ youth, which we will be updating as more services and resources emerge. You can also find out more about the organizations and people profiled in this book. If you know of an organization or provider that we should include, please contact us via our website (www.transkidsourkids.org).

Acknowledgments

This book would not have been possible without the support, guidance, and contributions of friends, colleagues, and mentors—as well as the generosity of the more than fifty interviewees who shared their stories with us.

First, we are exceedingly grateful to all the interviewees who participated in this project and entrusted us with their stories. Words cannot express how honored we are to be able to share them with the world.

Unending thanks go to two invaluable teammates from the Campaign for Southern Equality, Carolyn Jones and Liz Williams, who were excellent editors, brilliant thought partners, and indefatigable cheerleaders—and who stayed up many late nights with us to help cross the finish line on this project. Your intellectual contributions, kindness, and support mean the world to us. Thanks also to Liz for your beautiful cover design and for the leadership you provided to the online and artistic portions of this project.

We are deeply thankful to Robert Lasner at Ig Publishing for providing the creative spark for this project and your support throughout the publication process. Thank you for creating an invaluable space in which to share these remarkable stories.

Special thanks to our agent, Susan Ramer, for your support, thought partnership, guidance, and insights and your help shaping this project.

Thank you to the whole Campaign for Southern Equality staff, who provided terrific ideas regarding the shape and content of this book, and to the CSE leadership for your unwavering commitment to this project. The CSE team includes Van Bailey, Leila Barazandeh, Caty Cherepakhov, Emma Chinn, Kenya Cummings, Tiara Giddings, Chase Harless, Tavi Hawn, Ivy Hill, Austin Johnson, Carolyn Jones, Lore Lane, Hailee Mason, Christa Orth, Allison Scott, Holiday Simmons, Dorian Volpe, Craig White, and Liz Williams—and the board of directors, legal team, and consultants who make our work possible.

Thank you to Tavi Hawn and Holiday Simmons for helping us develop our Land Acknowledgment and for your key guidance and commitment to helping us share stories in ethical, inclusive, and culturally competent ways.

A special thanks to tilde Language Justice Co-op for providing Spanish-English interpretation services for interviews. Thank you also to Omni Romero for your translation assistance and support.

Many thanks to Reverend Art Wright, Alex McNeill,

Angela Dallara, Tavi Hawn, Holiday Simmons, Silas, Noell, Finn, Tiffany, Rochelle, Rebecca, Kathy, and Hannah for helping connect us to incredible interviewees. Your help is greatly appreciated.

Finally, we express our deepest gratitude to our partners, families, and friends for their boundless support, understanding, and love throughout this endeavor. Your belief in and encouragement of us got us through our marathon writing process—and we couldn't have done any of this without you.

To our readers, we hope that in reading this book, you experience the joy we did in writing it—and that you are as moved as we were by the stories of all who are featured in it. We look forward to a future filled with trans magic and joy, and we hope you'll join us in making it so.

Notes

1. Mike Laws, "Why We Capitalize 'Black' (and Not 'White')," *Columbia Journalism Review*, June 16, 2020, https://www.cjr.org/analysis/capital-b-black-styleguide.php.
2. "White, White," *The Diversity Style Guide*, accessed May 8, 2024, https://www.diversitystyleguide.com/glossary/white-white/.
3. Ann Thúy Nguyễn and Maya Pendleton, "Recognizing Race in Language: Why We Capitalize 'Black' and 'White,'" Center for the Study of Social Policy, March 23, 2020, https://cssp.org/2020/03/recognizing-race-in-language-why-we-capitalize-black-and-white.

INTRODUCTION

1. "Title IX and Athletic Opportunities in K–12 Schools," US Department of Education Office for Civil Rights, February 2023, https://www2.ed.gov/about/offices/list/ocr/docs/ocr-k12-athletic-resource-202302.pdf.
2. Gallup, "LGBTQ+ Rights," *Gallup*, March 14, 2024, https://news.gallup.com/poll/1651/gay-lesbian-rights.aspx.
3. Lauren Gambino, "Poll Shows US Public Support for LGBTQ+ Protections Falling for First Time since 2015," *The Guardian*, March 12, 2024, https://www.theguardian.com/us-news/2024/mar/11/us-public-support-lgbtq-protection-falls.
4. "Mapping Attacks on LGBTQ Rights in US State Legislatures in 2023," American Civil Liberties Union, February 6, 2024, https://www.aclu.org/legislative-attacks-on-lgbtq-rights-2023.

5. Annette Choi, "Record Number of Anti-LGBTQ Bills Were Introduced in 2023," CNN, January 22, 2024, https://www.cnn.com/politics/anti-lgbtq-plus-state-bill-rights-dg/index.html.
6. "Mapping Attacks," American Civil Liberties Union.
7. Kate Sosin, "This Texas Family Is Being Investigated Because Their Child Is Trans: 'I Don't Know Where It's Safe,'" PBS Newshour, March 11, 2022, https://www.pbs.org/newshour/nation/this-texas-family-is-being-investigated-because-their-child-is-trans-i-dont-know-where-its-safe.
8. Nicole Chavez, "A Florida School Board Member Filed a Criminal Complaint over a Black Queer Memoir," CNN, November 18, 2021, https://www.cnn.com/2021/11/17/us/florida-flagler-county-schools-all-boys-arent-blue-book/index.html.
9. Moriah Balinget, "Kentucky Banned Its Only Transgender Student-Athlete from Playing," *The Washington Post*, April 25, 2022, https://www.washingtonpost.com/education/2022/08/25/fischer-wells-trans-athlete-kentucky.
10. Adam Nagourney and Jeremy W. Peters, "How a Campaign against Transgender Rights Mobilized Conservatives," *The New York Times*, April 16, 2023, https://www.nytimes.com/2023/04/16/us/politics/transgender-conservative-campaign.html.
11. Katy Steinmetz, "The Transgender Tipping Point," *Time Magazine*, May 29, 2014, https://time.com/135480/transgender-tipping-point/.
12. Alexa Keefe, "'Gender Revolution' Portrait Carries Message of Hope," *National Geographic*, December 27, 2016, https://www.nationalgeographic.com/photography/article/robin-hammond-gender-cover.
13. Justin McCarthy, "U.S. Same-Sex Marriage Support Holds at 71% High," Gallup, June 5, 2023, https://news.gallup.com/poll/506636/sex-marriage-support-holds-high.aspx.
14. Patrick Boyle, "What Is Gender-Affirming Care?," American Association of Medical Colleges, accessed April 15, 2024, https://www.aamc.org/news/what-gender-affirming-care-your-questions-answered.

CHAPTER ONE

1. Jo Yurcaba and Associated Press, "Oklahoma Governor Signs Bill Withholding Hospital Funding over Trans Youth Care," NBC

News, October 5, 2022, https://www.nbcnews.com/nbc-out/out-politics-and-policy/oklahoma-governor-signs-bill-withholding-hospital-funding-trans-youth-rcna50804.

2. The bans on gender-affirming care usually threaten medical providers' licenses—so even if a healthcare provider offers telehealth services from a state without a ban, they cannot offer virtual care to patients who are physically in "ban states."

3. Bruce Schreiner and Dylan Lovan, "Kentucky's Ban on Gender-Affirming Care Takes Effect as Federal Judge Lifts Injunction," *PBS*, July 15, 2023, https://www.pbs.org/newshour/politics/kentuckys-ban-on-gender-affirming-care-takes-effect-as-federal-judge-lifts-injunction.

4. Eleanor Klibanoff and Alex Nguyen, "Austin Doctors Who Treated Trans Kids Leaving Dell Children's Clinic after Ag Paxton Announces Investigation," *The Texas Tribune*, May 13, 2023, https://www.texastribune.org/2023/05/13/austin-dell-childrens-gender-affirming.

CHAPTER TWO

1. Patrick Boyle, "What Is Gender-Affirming Care?," American Association of Medical Colleges, https://www.aamc.org/news/what-gender-affirming-care-your-questions-answered.

2. Chase Harless et al., *The Report of the 2019 Southern LGBTQ Health Survey*, 2019, https://southernequality.org/wp-content/uploads/2019/11/SouthernLGBTQHealthSurvey%E2%80%93FullReport.pdf.

3. Harless et al., *2019 Southern LGBTQ Health Survey*.

4. Jaime M. Grant et al., "Injustice at Every Turn: A Report of the National Transgender Discrimination Survey," Transequality, 2017, https://transequality.org/sites/default/files/docs/resources/NTDS_Report.pdf.

5. Pseudonym.

6. Diana M. Tordoff et al., "Mental Health Outcomes in Transgender and Nonbinary Youths Receiving Gender-Affirming Care," *JAMA Network Open* 5, no. 2 (February 25, 2022): e220978–e220978, https://doi.org/10.1001/jamanetworkopen.2022.0978.

7. Jack L. Turban et al., "Access to Gender-Affirming Hormones

during Adolescence and Mental Health Outcomes among Transgender Adults," *PLOS ONE* 17, no. 1 (January 12, 2022), https://doi.org/10.1371/journal.pone.0261039.

8. Jenifer K. McGuire et al., "Body Image in Transgender Young People: Findings from a Qualitative, Community Based Study," *Body Image* 18 (September 1, 2016): 96–107, https://doi.org/10.1016/j.bodyim.2016.06.004.

9. Asa Hutchinson, "Opinion | Asa Hutchinson: Why I Vetoed the GOP's Bill Restricting Transgender Youth Healthcare," *The Washington Post*, April 8, 2021, https://www.washingtonpost.com/opinions/asa-hutchinson-veto-transgender-health-bill-youth/2021/04/08/990c43f4-9892-11eb-962b-78c1d8228819_story.

10. Andrew Demillo, "Judge Rules Arkansas Ban on Gender-Affirming Care for Transgender Minors Violates US Constitution," AP News, April 11, 2024, https://apnews.com/us-news/arkansas-gender-general-news-2a0d032f4e4f3195c180d879239e6521.

11. Andrew Demillo and Jim Salter, "Federal Appeals Court Hears Arguments on Nation's First Ban in Gender-Affirming Care for Minors," AP News, April 11, 2024, https://apnews.com/article/transgender-gender-affirming-care-arkansas-court-c299aa1db823fded-a5b1e0b457a7a9b5.

12. Mickey Doyle, "Gender-Affirming Care Again Target of GOP Bills," *Arkansas Democrat Gazette*, January 14, 2024, https://www.arkansasonline.com/news/2024/jan/14/gender-affirming-care-again-target-of-gop-bills.

13. Minami Funakoshi and Disha Raychaudhuri, "The Rise of Anti-Trans Bills in the US," Reuters, August 19, 2023, https://www.reuters.com/graphics/USA-HEALTHCARE/TRANS-BILLS/zgvorreyapd.

14. Casey Parks, "After Mississippi Banned His Hormone Shots, an 8-Hour Journey," *The Washington Post*, July 28, 2023, https://www.washingtonpost.com/dc-md-va/interactive/2023/mississippi-youth-transgender-care-ban-aftermath.

15. Jemma Stephenson, "Federal Appeals Court Allows Alabama's Gender-affirming Care Ban to go into Effect," *Alabama Reflector*, January 11, 2024, https://alabamareflector.com/2024/01/11/federal-appeals-court-allows-alabamas-gender-affirming-care-ban-to-

go-into-effect/#:~:text=A%20federal%20court%20Thursday%20allowed,lower%20court%20ruling%20blocking%20it.

16. "Medical Organization Statements," Transgender Legal Defense and Education Fund, accessed May 8, 2024, https://transhealthproject.org/resources/medical-organization-statements/.

17. Human Rights Campaign Foundation, "Get the Facts on Gender-Affirming Care," HRC, July 25, 2023, https://www.hrc/org/resources/get-the-facts-on-gender-affirming-care

18. AP Staff Reports, "Protesters at W.Va. Capitol Rally against Proposed Gender-Affirming Care Ban," WCHS TV, March 10, 2023, https://wchstv.com/news/local/protesters-at-wva-capitol-rally-against-proposed-gender-affirming-care-ban.

19. MSNBC, "Chris Hayes Podcast with Dr. Izzy Lowell | Why Is This Happening? - EP 163" MSNBC, YouTube, May 27, 2021, video, 49:02, http://www.youtube.com/watch?v=Ej8JpoWMp3A.

CHAPTER THREE

1. Aliyya Swaby and Mollie Simon, "SC Hospital Bends to Political Pressure on Trans Healthcare," ProPublica, December 6, 2023, https://www.propublica.org/article/musc-medical-university-south-carolina-trans-healthcare-emails.

2. Azeen Ghorayshi, "Texas Youth Gender Clinic Closed Last Year under Political Pressure," *The New York Times*, March 8, 2022, https://www.nytimes.com/2022/03/08/health/texas-transgender-clinic-genecis-abbott.html.

3. Molly Minta, "Facing Political Pressure, UMMC Cut Care to Trans Kids before the Legislature Banned Doing so, Emails Show," *Mississippi Today*, September 6, 2023, https://mississippitoday.org/2023/04/26/facing-political-pressure-ummc-cut-care-to-trans-kids-before-the-legislature-banned-doing-so-emails-show/.

4. Jensen Matar, "I Am Transgender and I Belong Here," American Civil Liberties Union, April 7, 2017, https://www.aclu-ms.org/en/news/i-am-transgender-and-i-belong-here.

5. Courtney Ann Jackson, "Families and Advocates Rally Against Anti-Transgender Bill at the State Capitol," WLBT3, February 15, 2023, https://www.wlbt.com/2023/02/16

families-advocates-rally-against-anti-transgender-bill-state-capitol/
6. Jackson, "Families and Advocates Rally."
7. Casey Parks, "A Mississippi Mother Drove 8 Hours for Her Trans Son's Hormone Shots," *The Washington Post*, July 28, 2023, https://www.washingtonpost.com/dc-md-va/interactive/2023/mississippi-youth-transgender-care-ban-aftermath/.
8. Kentucky State Legislature, Senate Bill 150 (Session 2023), accessed June 7, 2024, https://legiscan.com/KY/text/SB150/2023.
9. Gabrilea Szymonowska, "Transgender Woman Who Died in Jackson Shooting Is Remembered for Learning To Accept Herself," *The Clarion-Ledger*, March 10, 2021, https://www.clarionledger.com/story/news/local/2021/03/11/friends-black-transgender-woman-killed-jackson-had-life-cut-short/4423312001.

CHAPTER FOUR

1. Defense of Marriage Act, H.R.3396, 104th Congress (1996).
2. "United States v. Windsor (Challenging the Federal 'Defense of Marriage Act')," New York Civil Liberties Union, accessed April 13, 2024, https://www.nyclu.org/en/cases/united-states-v-windsor-challenging-federal-defense-marriage-act.
3. "Mapping Attacks on LGBTQ Rights in US State Legislatures in 2023," American Civil Liberties Union, February 6, 2024, https://www.aclu.org/legislative-attacks-on-lgbtq-rights-2023.
4. Lindsey Dawson and Jennifer Kates, "Policy Tracker: Youth Access to Gender Affirming Care and State Policy Restrictions," KFF, April 9, 2024, https://www.kff.org/other/dashboard/gender-affirming-care-policy-tracker.
5. "Poe v. Labrador," American Civil Liberties Union, April 4, 2024, https://www.aclu.org/cases/poe-v-labrador.
6. Clint Hendler, "A Judge Just Blocked the Texas Law Allowing Vigilante Anti-Abortion Enforcement," *Mother Jones*, August 5, 2023, https://www.motherjones.com/politics/2023/08/texas-abortion-sb8-vigilante.
7. Alexia Korberg, "Opinion | Texas's Antiabortion Law Isn't

the First to Empower the Mob — and It Won't Be the Last," *The Washington Post*, September 9, 2021, https://www.washingtonpost.com/opinions/2021/09/09/texass-antiabortion-law-isnt-first-empower-mob-it-wont-be-last.

8. Ken Paxton, "AG Paxton Declares So-Called Sex-Change Procedures on Children and Prescription of Puberty Blockers to Be 'Child Abuse' Under Texas Law," Attorney General of Texas news release, February 21, 2022, https://www.texasattorneygeneral.gov/news/releases/ag-paxton-declares-so-called-sex-change-procedures-children-and-prescription-puberty-blockers-be.

9. "PFLAG v. Abbott," American Civil Liberties Union, April 3, 2024, https://www.aclu.org/cases/pflag-v-abbott.

10. Caitlin O'Kaine, "Tearful Mother Urges Texas Lawmakers Not to Pass Bill That Would Classify Supporting Transgender Children As Abuse," CBS News, April 16, 2021, https://Www.Cbsnews.Com/News/Texas-Transgender-Bill-Mother-Urges-Lawmakers-Not-To-Pass/?Ftag=YHF4eb9d17.

11. "PFLAG v. Office of the Attorney General of Texas," American Civil Liberties Union, May 3, 2024, https://www.aclu.org/cases/pflag-v-office-of-the-attorney-general-of-texas.

12. "About Us," PFLAG, accessed April 15, 2024, https://pflag.org/about-us.

13. "PFLAG v. Office of the Attorney General of Texas," American Civil Liberties Union.

14. "Families Block Idaho Law Banning Healthcare for Transgender Youth," American Civil Liberties Union, December 27, 2023, https://www.aclu.org/press-releases/families-block-idaho-law-banning-health-care-for-transgender-youth.

15. Poe v. Labrador, 1:23-cv-00269-BLW (D. Idaho 2023).

CHAPTER FIVE

1. Andy Rose and Paul LeBlanc, "Oklahoma GOP Governor Signs Anti-Transgender Bathroom Bill into Law," CNN, May 26, 2022, https://www.cnn.com/2022/05/25/politics/oklahoma-anti-transgender-bathroom-law-signed-stitt.

2. Rose and LeBlanc, "Oklahoma GOP."
3. Rose and LeBlanc, "Oklahoma GOP."
4. Sunnivie Brydum, "Texas Doubles down on Transphobic Legislation, Adding $2,000 Fine for 'Wrong' Bathroom Use," Advocate.com, November 17, 2015, https://www.advocate.com/politics/transgender/2015/03/10/texas-doubles-down-transphobic-legislation-adding-2000-fine-wrong-ba.
5. Mitch Kellaway, "Texas Bill Would Jail Those Whose Chromosomes Don't Match the Restroom They're Using," Advocate.com, November 17, 2015, https://www.advocate.com/politics/transgender/2015/02/24/texas-bill-would-jail-those-whose-chromosomes-dont-match-restroom-th.
6. Lauren Fox, "Bathroom Bill Another Way to 'Bully' Transgender Kids, Mothers Say," *Dallas News*, August 25, 2019, https://www.dallasnews.com/news/politics/2017/06/21/bathroom-bill-another-way-to-bully-transgender-kids-mothers-say.
7. Amber Briggle, "This is my transgender son in TEARS," Facebook, July 20, 2017, https://www.facebook.com/amberbriggle/photos/a.1605433579678191.1073741834/a.1605433579678191.1073741834.1592110124343870/1996734317214780/?type=3&theater.
8. Bradley Backburn, "Transgender Boy Gets New Birth Certificate," WFAA, 2017, https://www.wfaa.com/article/news/transgender-denton-boy-gets-new-birth-certificate/287-429411192.
9. "Anti-LGBTQ+ Bills That Are Impacting Children, Families and Schools," ADL, April 27, 2023, https://www.adl.org/resources/tools-and-strategies/anti-lgbtq-bills-are-impacting-children-families-and-schools.
10. "2023 Anti-LGBTQ Laws in the Classroom," The Point Foundation, July 14, 2023, https://pointfoundation.org/community/blog/2023-anti-lgbtq-laws.
11. Jo Yurcaba, "Over 30 New LGBTQ Education Laws Are in Effect As Students Go Back to School," NBC News, August 30, 2023, https://www.nbcnews.com/nbc-out/out-politics-and-policy/30-new-lgbtq-education-laws-are-effect-students-go-back-school-

rcna101897.
12. "Mapping Attacks on LGBTQ Rights in US State Legislatures in 2024," American Civil Liberties Union, accessed April 12, 2024, https://www.aclu.org/legislative-attacks-on-lgbtq-rights-2024.
13. Lilah Jacobs, "Know Your Rights: Back to School Edition," ACLU of Oklahoma, August 16, 2023, https://www.acluok.org/en/news/know-your-rights-back-school-edition.
14. Jacobs, "Know Your Rights."
15. Jacobs, "Know Your Rights."
16. Kaylee Olivas, "'Woke Olympics': OSDE Makes Permanent Rule To Prohibit School Districts from Altering Students' Gender Records," KFOR, January 25, 2024, https://kfor.com/news/local/woke-olympics-osde-makes-permanent-rule-to-prohibit-school-districts-from-altering-students-gender-records.
17. Olivas, "'Woke Olympics.'"
18. Alexia Aston, "Oklahoma Legislature Considering over 50 Bills Targeting LGBTQ+ Issues. What Do They Say?," *The Oklahoman*, February 20, 2024, https://www.oklahoman.com/story/news/politics/2024/02/20/oklahoma-legislature-considering-54-bills-targeting-lgbtq-issues-list/72597155007.
19. "Mapping Attacks," American Civil Liberties Union.
20. Jo Yurcaba, "Oklahoma Students Walk Out after Trans Student's Death to Protest Bullying Policies," NBC News, February 26, 2024, https://www.nbcnews.com/nbc-out/out-news/nex-benedict-death-protest-bullying-owasso-oklahoma-rcna140501.
21. C. Mandler, "What Happened to Nex Benedict?," NPR, March 22, 2024, https://www.npr.org/2024/03/15/1238780699/nex-benedict-nonbinary-oklahoma-death-bullying.
22. Jose Soto, "Honoring Nex Benedict, a 16-Year-Old Non-Binary Oklahoma High School Student Who Tragically Died One Day after Being Beaten Unconscious in a School Bathroom," Human Rights Campaign, February 21, 2024, https://www.hrc.org/news/honoring-nex-benedict-16-year-old-non-binary-high-school-student-who-tragically-died-after-school-beating.
23. "Native Land Rights and the Land Runs of 1891," Citizen

Potawatomi Nation, November 18, 2020, https://www.potawatomi.org/blog/2020/11/18/native-land-rights-and-the-land-runs-of-1891/#:~:text=You%20had%20Sooners%20who%20were,22%2C%2023%20and%2028.

24. "Land Run," The Chickasaw Nation Source Site, accessed April 13, 2024, https://chickasawfilmsource.com/Home/Entries/Events/Land-Run.aspx.

25. "Rushes to Statehood: The Oklahoma Land Runs," The National Cowboy and Western Heritage Museum, accessed April 13, 2024, https://chickasawfilmsource.com/Home/Entries/Events/Land-Run.aspx.

26. Levi Rickert, "NCAI Faces Controversial Constitutional Amendments to Remove State Recognized Tribes," Native News Online, November 14, 2023, https://nativenewsonline.net/sovereignty/ncai-faces-controversial-constitutional-amendments-to-remove-state-recognized-tribes.

27. Harlan Pruden, "Standing in Support of our Two Spirit Relatives in our Communities and Nations," National Congress of American Indians, 2015, https://archive.ncai.org/resources/resolutions/standing-in-support-of-our-two-spirit-relatives-in-our-communities-and-nations.

28. "Creation of Two Spirit Task Force," National Congress of American Indians, 2016, https://archive.ncai.org/PHX-16-046_draft.pdf.

29. Joe Killian, "Monday Numbers: North Carolina and the National Anti-LGBTQ Wave," NC Newsline, August 21, 2023, https://ncnewsline.com/2023/08/21/monday-numbers-north-carolina-and-the-national-anti-lgbtq-wave.

30. Ian Millhiser, "Florida's 'Don't Say Gay' Bill Is Unconstitutional," Vox, March 15, 2022, https://www.vox.com/2022/3/15/22976868/dont-say-gay-florida-unconstitutional-ron-desantis-supreme-court-first-amendment-schools-parents.

31. Stephanie Sy and Shoshana Dubnow, "What Florida's 'Don't Say Gay' Settlement Changes and What Restrictions Remain," PBS Newshour, March 14, 2024, https://www.pbs.org/newshour/show/what-floridas-dont-say-gay-settlement-changes-and-what-restrictions-remain.

32. Millhiser, "Florida's 'Don't Say Gay Bill.'"

33. North Carolina General Assembly, Senate Bill 49 (Session 2023), accessed April 15, 2024, https://www.ncleg.gov/Sessions/2023/Bills/

Senate/PDF/S49v4.pdf.

34. "BBC News with Katty and Christian, Jeff and Harleigh on Bills Banning Gender-Affirming Care," BBC News, April 2021, https://www.bbc.co.uk/programmes/p09ct4mn.

35. "Families Sue Alabama over Felony Ban on Gender-Affirming Care for Transgender Adolescents," American Civil Liberties Union, April 10, 2022, https://www.aclu.org/press-releases/families-sue-alabama-over-felony-ban-gender-affirming-care-transgender-adolescents.

36. Brian Woodham, "City Honors Auburn Teen with Proclamation," *The Auburn Villager*, November 30, 2023, https://www.auburn-villager.com/news/city-honors-auburn-teen-with-proclamation/article_da029e40-8975-11ee-8786-a3ca19ebe68b.

37. Alex Woodward, "Transgender Teen Defends Trans Rights in Senate Testimony: 'These Are Human Rights Hanging in The Balance,'" *The Independent*, June 21, 2023, https://www.the-independent.com/news/world/americas/us-politics/harleigh-walker-transgender-rights-senate-b2361803.

38. "Home," The GenderCool Project, accessed April 14, 2024, https://gendercool.org.

39. The Trevor Project, "2023 US National Survey on the Mental Health of LGBTQ Young People," 2023, https://www.thetrevorproject.org/survey-2023/assets/static/05_TREVOR05_2023survey.pdf.

40. "The Trevor Project Research Brief: Accepting Adults Reduce Suicide Attempts Among LGBTQ Youth," June 2019, https://www.thetrevorproject.org/wp-content/uploads/2019/06/Trevor-Project-Accepting-Adult-Research-Brief_June-2019.pdf.

CHAPTER SIX

1. Nikki Ross, "Student Organizer of FL's 'Don't Say Gay' School Walkout Suspended from Flagler School," *Daytona Beach News-Journal* Online, March 3, 2022, https://www.news-journalonline.com/story/news/education/2022/03/03/dont-say-gay-flagler-palm-coast-high-school-walkout-organizer-jack-petocz-suspended-indefinitely/9344494002/.

2. S. E. Smith, "Why It's a Mistake to Call Those Anti-LGBTQ

Laws 'Don't Say Gay,'" *TIME Magazine*, April 22, 2022, https://time.com/6169659/dont-say-gay-trans-youth.

3. "Florida Censorship Attempts," Florida Freedom to Read Project, accessed April 13, 2024, https://www.fftrp.org/florida_censorship_attempts.

4. Ariana Figueroa, "First Amendment Advocates Fight Growing Number of U.S. Book Bans," Nebraska Examiner, October 9, 2023, https://nebraskaexaminer.com/2023/10/09/first-amendment-advocates-fight-growing-number-of-u-s-book-bans/#:~:text=For%20the%202022%2D23%20school,281%3B%20and%20Pennsylvania%20with%20186.

5. Casey Kuhn, "Attempts to Ban Books Are at an All-Time High. These Librarians Are Fighting Back," PBS Newshour, April 11, 2024, https://www.pbs.org/newshour/arts/attempts-to-ban-books-are-at-an-all-time-high-these-librarians-are-fighting-back.

6. "American Library Association Reports Record Number of Unique Book Titles Challenged in 2023," American Library Association, March 14, 2024, https://www.ala.org/news/press-releases/2024/03/american-library-association-reports-record-number-unique-book-titles.

7. Kasey Meehan et al., "Banned in the USA: Narrating the Crisis," PEN America, April 16, 2024, https://pen.org/report/narrating-the-crisis.

8. "Three Percenters," Southern Poverty Law Center, accessed April 13, 2024, https://www.splcenter.org/fighting-hate/extremist-files/group/three-percenters.

9. "Proud Boys," ADL, accessed April 13, 2024, https://www.adl.org/resources/backgrounder/proud-boys-0.

10. "About GLSEN," GLSEN, accessed April 14, 2024, https://www.glsen.org.

11. Jack Petocz, "Today, the florisa House passed the "Don't Say Gay' bill, February 24, 2022, 5:10 p.m., https://twitter.com/Jack_Petocz/status/1496970919293632513.

12. Matt Lavietes, "Florida Students Stage School Walkouts Over 'Don't Say Gay' Bill," NBC News, March 3, 2022, https://www.nbcnews.com/nbc-out/out-politics-and-policy/florida-students-stage-school-walkouts-dont-say-gay-bill-rcna18600

13. "Students Fight Anti-LGBTQ Policies with Nationwide Walkouts," GLAAD, September 28, 2022, https://glaad.org/students-fight-anti-lgbtq-policies-nationwide-walkouts.
14. "Mission and Vision," Queer Youth Assemble, 2023, https://queeryouthassemble.org/mission-vision.
15. "2015 US Transgender Survey: Florida State Report," Transequality, Washington, DC: National Center for Transgender Equality, 2017, https://transequality.org/sites/default/files/docs/usts/USTSFLStateReport(1017).

CHAPTER SEVEN

1. Clifford Rosky, "Anti-Gay Curriculum Laws," *Columbia Law Review* 117, no. 6 (October 2017), https://doi.org/https://columbialawreview.org/content/anti-gay-curriculum-laws.
2. Gender and Sexuality Alliance v. Spearman, 2:20-cv-00847-DCN (DSC 2020), https://southernequality.org/wp-content/uploads/2020/02/2020.02.26-Complaint.pdf February 26, 2020.
3. Consent Decree and Judgment, Gender and Sexuality Alliance v. Spearman, 2:20-cv-00847-DCN (DSC 2020), https://ed.sc.gov/state-board/state-board-of-education/about-state-board/gender-equity-lawsuit-final-order-march-11-2020.
4. "Grimm v. Gloucester County School Board," American Civil Liberties Union, October 6, 2021, https://www.aclu.org/cases/grimm-v-gloucester-county-school-board.
5. Katy Steinmetz, "The Transgender Tipping Point," *TIME Magazine*, May 29, 2014, https://time.com/135480/transgender-tipping-point/.
6. Richard Fausset, "Bathroom Law Repeal Leaves Few Pleased in North Carolina," *The New York Times*, March 30, 2017, https://www.nytimes.com/2017/03/30/us/north-carolina-senate-acts-to-repeal-restrictive-bathroom-law.html.
7. Harry Enten, "Republican Senators Aren't Embracing Trump's Transgender Military Ban," *FiveThirtyEight*, July 26, 2017, https://fivethirtyeight.com/features/republican-senators-arent-embracing-trumps-transgender-military-ban.

8. Freedom for All Massachusetts, "Mother of a Transgender Child Calls for Full Non-Discrimination," Facebook, February 16, 2016, https://www.facebook.com/FreedomMassachusetts/videos/1555907444720331.

9. Lisa Creamer, "Mass. Votes 'Yes' on Question 3 To Keep Law Protecting Transgender People in Public Accommodations," WBUR News, November 6, 2018, https://www.bur.org/news/2018/11/06/question-3-transgender-ballot-yes-wins.

10. Merriam-Webster.com Dictionary, s.v. "deadname," accessed April 14, 2024, https://www.merriam-webster.com/dictionary/deadname.

11. Ashton Mota, *A Kids Book About Being Inclusive* (New York, NY: DK Publishing, 2021).

12. Lindsay Morris, photographer, and Ruth Padawer, author, "The Kids of Camp I Am, a Decade Later," *The New York Times*, August 10, 2021, https://www.nytimes.com/interactive/2021/08/10/magazine/camp-i-am.html.

13. Fan Liang, "Top Surgery (Chest Feminization or Chest Masculinization)," Johns Hopkins University, accessed April 14, 2024, https://www.hopkinsmedicine.org/health/treatment-tests-and-therapies/top-surgery.

CHAPTER EIGHT

1. Blair Sabol, "Health Advisory Committee Members Blindsided by Board Decision to Remove Them," Live 5 News, October 6, 2023, https://www.live5news.com/2023/10/06/health-advisory-committee-members-blindsided-by-board-decision-remove-them.

2. "2023 US National Survey on the Mental Health of LGBTQ Young People," The Trevor Project, accessed April 13, 2024, https://www.thetrevorproject.org/survey-2023.

CHAPTER NINE

1. Rachel Sandler, "Arkansas Passes Anti-Trans Healthcare Bill After Lawmakers Override Veto," *Forbes*, April 6, 2021, https://www.forbes.com/sites/rachelsandler/2021/04/06/arkansas-passes-anti-trans-healthcare-bill-after-lawmakers-override-veto/?sh=4dc2649e26fa.

2. "Montana Two-Spirit Gathering," Montana Two-Spirit Society,

accessed April 14, 2024, https://www.mttwospirit.org/mt-two-spirit-gathering.

3. Anya Montiel, "LGBTQIA+ Pride and Two-Spirit People," *Smithsonian Magazine*, June 23, 2021, https://www.smithsonian-mag.com/blogs/national-museum-american-indian/2021/06/23/lgbtqia-pride-and-two-spirit-people.

4. "Two-Spirit," Indian Health Services, accessed April 14, 2024, https://www.ihs.gov/lgbt/health/twospirits.

5. Danielle Harrison, "Tribal Member Named Mr. Montana Two Spirit," *Smoke Signals*, November 15, 2021, https://www.smokesignals.org/articles/2021/11/15/tribal-member-named-mr-montana-two-spirit/.

6. "Home," Bay Area American Indian Two-Spirits, accessed April 12, 2024, https://www.baaits.org.

7. Kaili Berg, "Bay Area's Trailblazing Two-Spirit Organization Turns 25," Native News Online, February 22, 2024, https://nativenewsonline.net/arts-entertainment/bay-area-s-trailblazing-two-spirit-organization-turns-25.

8. Jovonne Wagner, "This Is Medicine: Montana Two-Spirit Society Host Gathering," ICT News, https://ictnews.org/news/this-is-medicine-montana-two-spirit-society-host-gathering.

9. Bryan Newland, "Federal Indian Boarding School Initiative Investigative Report,"U.S. Department of the Interior, May 2022, https://www.bia.gov/sites/default/files/dup/inline-files/bsi_investigative_report_may_2022_508.pdf.

10. Olivia X. Waxman, "The History of Native American Boarding Schools Is Even More Complicated Than a New Report Reveals," *TIME Magazine*, https://time.com/6177069/american-indian-boarding-schools-history.

CHAPTER TEN

1. "Episode 4 - I Thought Something Was Wrong With Me," Kin•dom Campfire Chats, February 21, 2024, https://kindom.buzzsprout.com/2290029/14364305-episode-4-i-thought-something-was-wrong-with-me?t=0.

2. Pepa Paniagua, "Year Two for Kin•dom Camp!," Grace Presbytery, May 24, 2023, https://www.gracepresbytery.org/year-two-for-kin

%E2%88%99dom-camp.

3. "Youth Topics: LGBTQ+," Youth.gov, 2024, https://youth.gov/youth-topics/lgbt-0.

4. "LGBTQ+ Youth Homelessness and Housing Instability Statistics," The Trevor Project, February 15, 2022, https://www.thetrevorproject.org/research-briefs/homelessness-and-housing-instability-among-lgbtq-youth-feb-2022.

5. "Find an RIC Partner," Reconciling Works, December 7, 2023, https://www.reconcilingworks.org/ric/findric.

6. "Home," True Colors United, 2024, https://truecolorsunited.org/.

7. "Debra Hopkins," LGBTQ Religious Archives Network, July 2020, https://lgbtqreligiousarchives.org/profiles/debra-hopkins.

8. Transequality, "The Report of the 2015 US Transgender Survey Executive Summary," US Trans Survey, December 2017, https://www.ustranssurvey.org/reports.

9. "2015 US Transgender Survey,"

10. A Yiddish word meaning homelike, warm, and cozy.

11. Liam M. Hooper, *Trans-Forming Proclamation: A Transgender Theology of Daring Existence* (N.p.: OtherWise Engaged Publishing, 2020). This book is currently under revision and is no longer in print through OWE Publishing.

12. Karen McVeigh, "North Carolina Passes Amendment 1 Banning Same-Sex Unions," *The Guardian*, May 9, 2012, https://www.theguardian.com/world/2012/may/09/north-carolina-passes-amendment-1.

13. Ralph Ellis et al., "Orlando Shooting: 49 Killed, Shooter Pledged ISIS Allegiance," CNN, June 13, 2016, https://www.cnn.com/2016/06/12/us/orlando-nightclub-shooting.

ABOUT THE AUTHORS

Jasmine Beach-Ferrara is an ordained minister and Executive Director of the Campaign for Southern Equality. She is the author of *Damn Love*, a short story collection that received recognition from PEN/Hemingway. Her non-fiction and opinion writing about LGBTQ+ issues in the South have been published in regional and national digital and print media. She received her undergraduate degree from Brown University, her MFA from the Warren Wilson Program for Writers, and her MDiv from Harvard Divinity School. She lives in Asheville, North Carolina, with her family.

Adam Polaski serves as the Communications and Political Director for the Campaign for Southern Equality. Previously, he worked on the digital and communication teams at Freedom to Marry, the successful campaign to win marriage for same-sex couples across the United States, and Freedom for All Americans, a national organization committed to securing LGBTQ-inclusive nondiscrimination protections. Adam has been recognized for Excellence in Online Journalism by the National Lesbian and Gay Journalists Association. He graduated summa cum laude with a degree in journalism from Ithaca College. He lives in Asheville, North Carolina.

Alexis Stratton has an MFA in Creative Writing from the University of South Carolina. Their stories and essays have appeared in *Hayden's Ferry Review, Matador Review and Oyez Review*, among other publications. In 2023, they won the James River Writers' and Richmond Magazine's Best Unpublished Novel Contest. Alexis also writes for the *Rebel Girls* book series and podcast and provides grant writing support to several LGBTQ+ nonprofits. They currently live in Richmond, Virginia.